The *FIGHTING* COLOURS *of*

Richard J. Caruana
50th Anniversary Collection

5: Hawker Hunter

History

Concept, artwork, text and overall design:
  © *Richard J. Caruana*

Published by:
Wydawnictwo Stratus sp.j.
Żeromskiego 4
27-600 Sandomierz
Poland

To

Godfrey Mangion
*Friend, Colleague,
Brother in Aviation*

Acknowledgements:
Adrian Balch
Ray Deacon
Ronnie Olsthoorn
Stephen Murray
Steve Page
Paul Pendleton-Brown
Darren Prior
Chris Sandham-Bailey
Charles Stafrace
Mark Zerafa

Call it elegance, call it grace, or even beauty; Hawker's Hunter was the last of a breed of aircraft where one of the rules of thumb in design philosophy was 'if it looks right, it will fly right'. No computer gurus were around at that time, able to run simulated test runs on the desktop. It all had to be done by pencil and slide-rule.

The aerodynamic development scene of the immediate post-war era was characterised by sharp contrasts on either side of the Atlantic. Whereas the tempo of wartime research was to continue unabated in America, the British industry was led by Government into an austerity programme, convinced that the Gloster Meteor would serve well into the early 'fifties. In the United States, a very innovative aircraft was taking shape, one that would leave an indelible mark on fighter development, the North American F-86 Sabre.

At that time, Hawker Aircraft Ltd were absorbed by development work on the P.1040, which stemmed from the company's first jet design, the P.1035. Later to be called the Sea Hawk, it flew for the first time on 2 September 1947 and was eventually to enter service in March 1953. Intrigued by the possibility of

Hunter FR.10s of No 2 Squadron RAF, taking off from Luqa (Malta) on 23 July 1969. In the background is XE556/W, and XE626/I is in the foreground (Charles Stafrace)

designing a Sabre competitor, Hawker handed over the Sea Hawk production programme to Armstrong Whitworth in order to concentrate on responding to Air Ministry Specification F.43/46. This called for a single-seat fighter powered by an axial-flow jet engine as opposed to the centrifugal power-plants, then already reaching their development limitations.

Hawker's Chief Designer, Sir Sydney Camm found little inspiration in the official specifications as outlined in F.43/46 and gave birth to a completely different design concept under the designation of P.1067. The design was flexible enough to accept different power plants, initial considerations being given to the Rolls Royce AJ.65 (later the Avon) or the Metrovick F.9 (taken over later on by Armstrong Whitworth and named Sapphire).

Specification F.3/48 was written around Hawker's proposal, superseding F.43/46. According to standard practice of the time, the specification was also presented to Vickers-Supermarine. This led to the birth of the Swift, a difficult machine that enjoyed a very short service life. By that time it was clear that duplication of such projects was wasteful in resources and enormously expensive; competitive fly-offs became a thing of the past, at least in Britain.

Hawker received an order for three prototypes in June 1948, two of which were to be powered by the Avon and the third by the Sapphire. Here again, duplication of power plant was an essential consideration as both engines were still unknown quantities. This, however, most probably served to save the live of Camm's new fighter, as will be seen later on.

The earliest configuration of Hawker's design featured a nose intake, mid-fuselage swept wings and a 'T' tailplane. Camm revised his idea about the nose opting for a bifurcated intake in the wing roots similar to that of the Sea Hawk. Swept wing development had already been going on for some time at Hawker's, with the P.1052 and the P.1081 being flown for the first time on 19 September 1948 and 19 June 1950 respectively. This programme was by no means uneventful: on 3 April 1951, Chief Test Pilot, Squadron Leader (Sqdn Ldr) 'Wimpey' Wade, lost his life after diving in the P.1081, probably attempting a transonic dive on the experience he had gained on the F-86.

Meanwhile, great thought had gone into the fighter's armament installation, with Hawker introducing a self-contained gun-pack incorporating not only the four 30mm Aden cannon, but also the breeches and 150 rounds of ammunition per gun. The pack could be changed in the field in less than five minutes. A single pressure refuelling point, situated in the port undercarriage bay, enabled the fighter to be turned round within close to eight minutes.

As from September 1948, Hawkers began work on building a mock-up, and by the end of the following year preparations were in hand to begin cutting metal for the first prototype. "Instruction to Proceed" was in hand by March 1950,

enabling Hawkers to initiate production planning for 400 aircraft, equally divided between those to be powered by the Avon and Sapphire. Construction of the first prototype P.1067, named 'Hunter', was well advanced early in 1951. Well before the first flight, an initial contract for 113 examples had been placed on 14 March 1951.

Due to Wade's demise in April, flight testing of the Hunter programme became the responsibility of Sqdn Ldr Neville Duke, beginning with taxying trials of WB188. The prototype was transferred from Kingston to Boscombe Down, where Duke progressed to ever-higher speeds with each taxying run. The Hunter took to the air for the first time on 20 July 1951, for a flight of about an hour during which the test pilot flew the aircraft up to 20,000ft. Only a couple of months later, the prototype was shown publicly for the first time at the SBAC Show, Farnborough.

Second Avon prototype (WB195) performed its first flight on 3 May 1952, followed by the Sapphire-powered third prototype (WB202) on 30 November. By that time, the Avon-powered examples were designated F. Mk. 1 while the Sapphire-powered Hunters were to be known as F. Mk. 2s. Camm rightly believed that the Hunter possessed further development potential and forwarded

Hawker Hunter Mk 6 belonging to the production batch of seven aircraft with pre-Mod.228 Mk.4 wings, built by Hawker Aircraft Ltd Kingston-upon-Thames. It spent its development period with HAL and A&AEE for miscellaneous trials. In 1960 it was converted to FR. Mk.10 and eventually served with Nos IV and 2 Squadrons RAF (Photo: Hawker Aircraft Limited)

A pair of Hunters FR.Mk.10s from No IV Squadron RAF, display very interesting underside detail, particularly the position and style of underwing serials and national markings. Camouflage between XF438 (top) and XE580 differ slightly; note how the former has the top colours extended below the wing and tailplane leading edges. Colours of fuselage serials vary, those of XF438 are black, those of XE580 are white (RAF Germany HQ PR Office)

Quite a number of early series examples were used as development aircraft, with initial deliveries of F. Mk. 1s being delivered to the Central Flying Establishment, West Rayham; first front-line squadron to receive the type was No 43 Squadron at RAF Leuchars in July 1954. Later that same year, in October, it was the turn of No 222 Squadron with No 54 being the third (and last) F. Mk. 1 unit, receiving it new aircraft in February 1955 at Odiham.

Problems and Solutions

As was to be expected, the Hunter suffered its share of teething troubles. In fact, certain problems required detail redesign in certain areas, features which eventually appeared as standard on later marks. Rear buffeting was experienced but quickly cured with the introduction of a bullet fairing at the tailplane/rudder end junction. The acute rear-view restriction was only partially offset by a slight modification of the canopy. Other serious problems emerged, such as tailplane pitch-up at high Mach numbers.

Probably the most immediate and critical point was fuel shortage. The original internal tankage of 324 gallons (1473 litres) provided the Hunter with very short legs. Wing leading edge tanks were later introduced, partially easing the problem, but the thirsty Avon (and far more thirsty Sapphire) could only be quenched by the introduction of external tanks.

Pitch problems were eventually ironed out by the extension of the outer wing leading edges. The original theory that the wing flaps could double as air brakes did not work well and called for further elaboration. Attempts were made to install perforated flaps and fuselage side airbrakes, none of which were considered acceptable. A solution was finally found in installing a ventral airbrake under the rear fuselage. This came as a 'bolt-on' unit and remained so from the 20th production aircraft onwards, no effort being made to incorporate this feature within the airframe!

The 'Achilles Heel' of the Hunter was to be its four-cannon armament. The earliest gun firing trials had been positively conducted with a Sapphire-engined Hunter, and this version was to be spared the troubles that plagued its Avon-powered partner. The latter engines would surge and flame-out whenever the guns were fired, as gasses from the breeches were ingested through the nearby air-intakes. It was only thanks to Rolls Royce's speedy intervention (and, to a certain extent, the total failure of the Supermarine Swift) that the Hunter was saved from the axe. The 200-series Avons featured a modified compressor that insured against engine surge problems. The Sapphire-engine version, on the other hand, would hardly have saved the Hunter, as it had already proved more expensive to produce and to operate.

As already mentioned, the gun pack design was a radical feature in itself. The only modifications in this area consisted in the addition of curved chutes for the shell cases and faired collectors (nicknamed 'Sabrinas') for their links, as some

his proposal of the P.1083, which featured higher wing sweep-back and an afterburning engine. This project, however, was cancelled the following year.

The Hunter recorded its first supersonic dive on 24 June 1952 and within a few months orders for the new fighter had reached a total of 550 examples. It was at this point that post-war neglect of the British aviation industry began to be felt, as tools, equipment and qualified personnel were difficult – if not impossible – to find. Gloster relinquished its order for 151 examples as it was incapable of producing them. Production plans set up three main centres; the main Hawker's works at Kingston and at Squires Gate (Blackpool) were assigned the Avon-powered versions, while Armstrong-Whitworth at Bitteswell catered for the Sapphire.

First production Hunter F. Mk. 1 (WT555) flew for the first time on 16 May 1953 piloted by Frank Murphy. The first Mk. 2 (WN888) which was assembled at Baginton flew on 14 October of that same year. Meanwhile, the original prototype (WB188) was fitted with an afterburning Avon RA.79R which provided 9,600lb (4,354kg) thrust, and lateral airbrakes on the rear end of the fuselage. In this form, it received the designation of F. Mk.3 and gained the world speed record on 7 September 1953 when Neville Duke clocked 727.63mph (1164.2km/h).

airframe damage had been experienced before these modifications had been introduced.

More Hunter Versions

Apart from the three front-line squadrons already mentioned, 25 Hunter F. Mk. 1s were delivered to No 229 Operational Conversion Unit (OCU) at Chivenor in 1955, with a second Hunter OCU (No 233) being established at Pembry the following year. Sapphire-powered F. Mk. 2s had, in the meantime, already entered service with No 257 Squadron in September 1954 followed by No 263 Squadron in January of the following year, forming the Wattisham Wing. Production of the F. Mk. 2 was cut back to the 45 examples shared by these two units.

Hawker's next version of the Hunter was the F. Mk. 4. This was the first version to introduce underwing hardpoints for the attachment of external 100-gallon (454 litres) fuel tanks. It was also fitted with the strengthened wing that, apart from incorporating internal leading edge fuel tanks, had additional hardpoints enabling it to carry a wide variety of stores, including bombs or rockets. The first of 356 examples of this mark was WT701. No less than 22 RAF squadrons were equipped with the type, particularly well known being No 111 Squadron that received its Mk.4s in June 1955. In their majority, these squadrons were ex-Sabres units based in Germany. Among those who received this mark of Hunter on the home front was No 54, replacing the Mk. 1s as its older machines were transferred to OCUs.

Next in line was the F. Mk.5, which incorporated all the new features introduced on the F. Mk. 4 while retaining the Sapphire Mk.101 of the earlier F Mk. 2. A total of 105 examples of this mark were built by Armstrong Whitworth at Coventry, the type entering service with No 56 Squadron at Waterbeach in May 1955 in replacement of the ill-fated Swift. The Hunter F. Mk. 5 enjoyed wider use, having also equipped Nos 1, 34, 41, 257 and 263 Squadrons. It is of interest to record that the last two squadrons mentioned did not dispose entirely of their F. Mk. 2s, but continued to fly them alongside the newer Mk. 5s well into 1957.

It was also this version of the Hunter to experience 'combat' operations when Nos 1 and 34 Squadrons were transferred to Nicosia (Cyprus) in October 1956 to participate in the Suez campaign. Daubed with yellow and black identification stripes, these Hunters flew strikes against Egypt on 1 November, but their limited range made their efforts ineffective. In fact, no air-to-air combats were reported; two Hunters were lost when they were blown up by EOKA terrorists.

A Real Hunter Emerges

Work on the P.1083, which had been 80 percent complete before being cancelled in July 1953, did not go to waste. Not enough development had been registered with the re-heat version of the Avon, so the possibility of an RA.19R-powered Hunter was dismissed. However, numerous components of the P.1083,

particularly those pertaining to the fuselage, were suitably modified and eventually flown as the P.1099. In this way, XF833 became the Hunter F. Mk.6 prototype, flying for the first time on 22 January 1954 from Dunsfold with Neville Duke at the controls.

'Bill' Bedford flew the first of seven development F. Mk. 6s (WW592-WW598) on 25 March 1955, this example being joined by all the other aircraft in the flight test programme by the end of that year. XE526, the first production F. Mk. 6, was flown by Hugh Merewether on 11 October 1955, with deliveries of the new mark to Maintenance Units (MU) beginning in January of the following year. The type's entry into squadron service had to be considerably delayed, however.

The Rolls Royce Avon 203 installed in this version provided some 30 percent extra thrust and had been certified against surging problems encountered with earlier marks. Pitch-up problems caused by the increase in power were soon ironed out with the introduction of a modified wing leading edge, featuring an extended outer section. This resulted in a 'saw-tooth' edge, a characteristic feature of all marks of Hunter that were to follow. During gun firing trials pitch-down problems were encountered, and these were eventually cured with the introduction of muzzle blast deflectors.

Solutions such as those mentioned above were introduced on the production lines when some 100 examples had already been built. However, these mods were retrospectively introduced not only to those Mk.6s already delivered, but also to a number of F. Mk. 4s still in service. A lot of valuable work had been undertaken at the MUs to bring the F. Mk. 6 up to standard, particularly No 5 at Kemble, No 19 at St Athan, No 33 at Lyneham and No 45 at Kinloss.

A pair of Hawker Hunters FGA. Mk. 9s at Luqa, Malta in 1971. The Hunter in the foreground is XE649/R. Both Hunters carry the markings of No 8 and 43 Squadrons, of the Khormaksar Strike Wing (Richard J. Caruana Collection)

Taking off from Runway 04 at RAF Luqa (Malta) is GA.11 XE685/861 on 12 October 1971 (Richard J. Caruana)

Fleet Requirements and Air Direction Unit Hunter T.8 WT799/839 taking off from RAF Luqa. These were often seen during cooperation exercises with Royal Navy ships in the Mediterranean (Godfrey Mangion)

First squadron to be equipped with the Hunter F. Mk. 6 was No 74 at Horsham St Faith. The re-equipment programme soon gained momentum, and the type formed the main equipment of 19 RAF front-line squadrons over the next few years. As the Hunter reached it peak of perfection, the infamous Duncan Sandys White Paper of 1957 (claiming that the days of the manned interceptor were numbered) brought about the cancellation of the last 150 F. Mk. 6s on order. Far more significant was the total cancellation of a number of extremely important projects then in hand. Eventually even TSR.2 was cancelled in April 1965.

A solo display by the Hunter could thrill crowds at any airshow, but that was nothing in comparison with the sight of 22 aircraft from No 111 Squadron in formation ('The Black Arrows') following their leader Sqdn Ldr Peter Latham in a perfect loop! On conversion of 111 Squadron to Lightnings in 1961, the task of providing the RAF with an official aerobatic team fell on No 92 Squadron, whose all-blue Hunters were appropriately name 'the Blue Diamonds'.

Regenerating the Hunter
The cancellation of remaining orders meant that Hunter production for the RAF ended with XK156 on 9 July 1957. This aircraft was to be the last single-seat

Hunter built for the RAF, all other versions that came later were rebuilt from earlier marks. The first such major conversion was initiated in 1958 when Hawker Aircraft Ltd were requested to convert 100 F. Mk. 6 Hunters to replace the ageing De Havilland Venom in the ground-attack role in the Middle East. Fitted with the Avon 207, the FGA. 9 also featured strengthened wings, increased oxygen capacity for longer flights and tropical equipment.

Immediately noticeable was a 'hump' added above the rear fuselage, housing a 13' 6" (4.15m) diameter braking parachute. Apart from retaining the four 30mm Aden cannon, this new version of the Hunter could pack quite a punch under its strengthened wings. Four underwing stations could carry up to two 1,000lb (450Kg) loads of ordnance each, including practice bomb carriers, 2" or 3" rockets in various configurations, or the standard 100 gallon (454 litre), apart from the new 230 gallon (1045 litre) drop tanks. The latter, carried under the inner pulons, was longer than previous drop tanks and necessitated a cut-out in the flaps, and their installation was undertaken at RAF MUs.

A reconnaissance role for the Hunter had been envisaged for quite some time, so much so that Hawkers had installed a five-camera nose on an F. Mk. 4 (WT780) as a private venture. This proposal earned the company a contract to convert 40 Hunters F. Mk. 6 to take a simpler, 3-camera nose, the first prototype (XF429) flying for the first time on 7 November 1959. First unit to receive the Hunter FR.10 was No IV Squadron in January 1961 followed by No 2, the following March, both based in Germany. No 1417 Flight at Khormaksar (1961-67) was the only one of the FR.10 units to fire its guns in anger. The Germany-based Hunters were eventually replaced during 1970 with Phantoms FGR. 2 (No 2) and Harriers GR. 1 (No IV).

The final single-seat version to appear was the navalised Hunter. During the early 1960s, Hawker was instructed to convert a batch of 40 F. Mk. 4 as single seat trainers for the Fleet Air Arm. Cannon armament was removed, gun troughs faired over, and 'Sabrinas' deleted. They also featured the 'saw-tooth' wing leading edge, which could also carry rocket launchers, or four 100 gallon underwing tanks, or a combination of both. In true navy fashion, it was fitted with an arrestor hook. In this form it was designated Hunter GA.11 and entered service in 1962. A few examples fitted with a camera nose similar to that of the FR.10 were known by the designation of PR. 11A.

Navy Hunters began their operations in 1962 with No 738 and 764 Naval Air Squadrons (NAS), their work being later taken over by the Fleet Requirements and Air Direction Unit (FRADU). The first Hunter GA.11 (WV267) for FRADU arrived at Hurn on 27 March 1969, the type enjoying a long operational life, being retired from service in 1995. During that time a powerful Harley Light was fitted in the nose. Apart from their mundane training duties, four of these Hunters also formed an aerobatic team, 'The Blue Herons'.

© RJC

Colour Art   *All Colour Art © Richard J. Caruana – 2024*

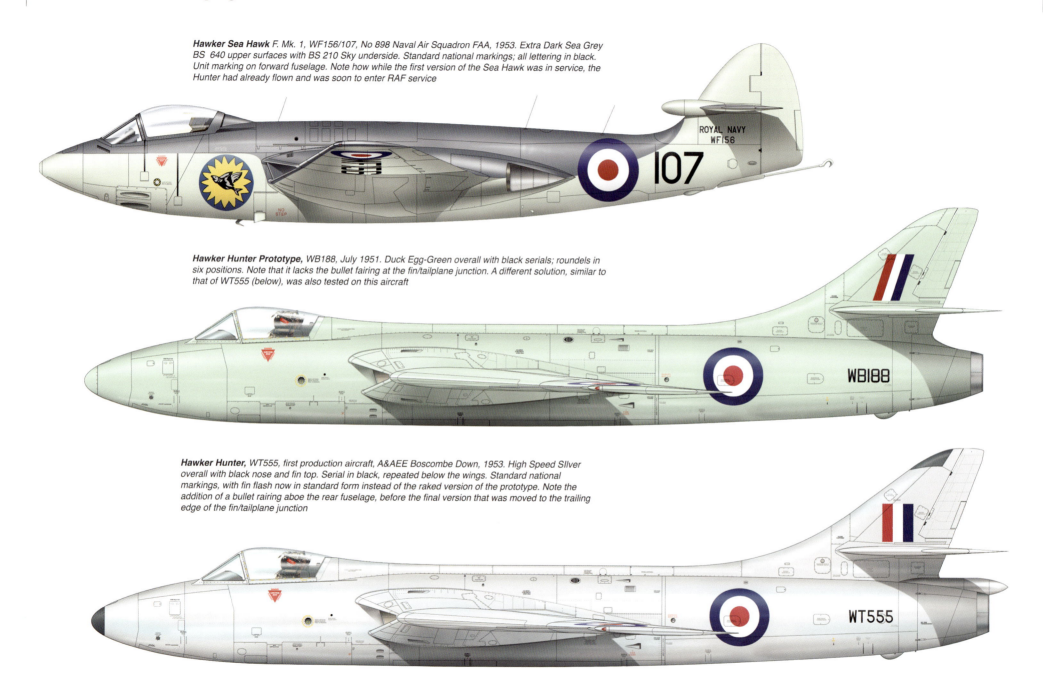

Hawker Sea Hawk *F. Mk. 1, WF156/107, No 898 Naval Air Squadron FAA, 1953. Extra Dark Sea Grey BS 640 upper surfaces with BS 210 Sky underside. Standard national markings; all lettering in black. Unit marking on forward fuselage. Note how while the first version of the Sea Hawk was in service, the Hunter had already flown and was soon to enter RAF service*

Hawker Hunter Prototype, *WB188, July 1951. Duck Egg-Green overall with black serials; roundels in six positions. Note that it lacks the bullet fairing at the fin/tailplane junction. A different solution, similar to that of WT555 (below), was also tested on this aircraft*

Hawker Hunter, *WT555, first production aircraft, A&AEE Boscombe Down, 1953. High Speed SIlver overall with black nose and fin top. Serial in black, repeated below the wings. Standard national markings, with fin flash now in standard form instead of the raked version of the prototype. Note the addition of a bullet rairing aboe the rear fuselage, before the final version that was moved to the trailing edge of the fin/tailplane junction*

Hawker Hunter *F. Mk.1, WT641/T, No 43 Squadron RAF, Leuchars, July 1954. Dark Sea Grey BS 638/Dark Green BS 641 upper surfaces with Aluminium undersides; black/white checks flanking fuselage roundels. Serial in black, white code 'T' on rear fuselage repeated on nose wheel door*

Hawker Hunter *F. Mk.1, WW645/S, No 43 Squadron RAF, 'Fighting Cocks', Leuchars, 1955. Dark Sea Grey BS 638/Dark Green BS 641 upper surfaces with Aluminium undersides; black/white checks flanking fuselage roundel. Black serial, repeated below wings; yellow code 'S' on rear fuselage, repeated on nose wheel door. Unit badge on nose. This was the last production F1*

Hawker Hunter *F. Mk.1, WT815/O, No 222 Squadron RAF, Leuchars, 1955. Dark Sea Grey BS 638/Dark Green BS 641 upper surfaces with Aluminium undersides; blue/red checks flanking fuselage roundel. Black serial, repeated below wings; white code 'O' on rear fuselage, repeated in black on nose-wheel door*

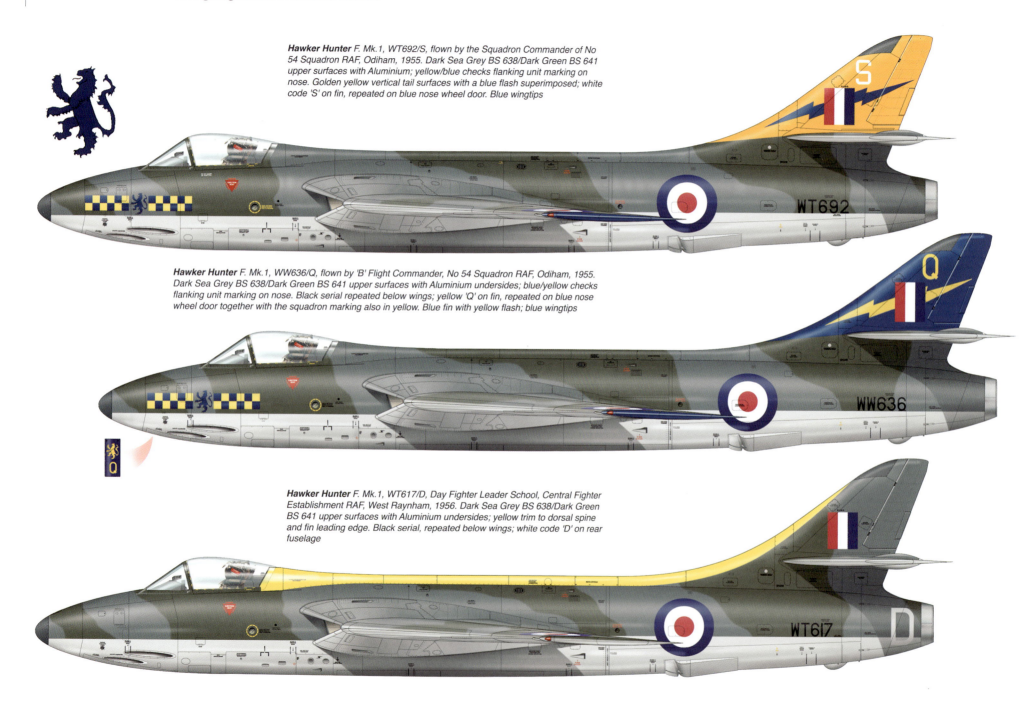

Hawker Hunter F. Mk.1, WT692/S, flown by the Squadron Commander of No 54 Squadron RAF, Odiham, 1955. Dark Sea Grey BS 638/Dark Green BS 641 upper surfaces with Aluminium; yellow/blue checks flanking unit marking on nose. Golden yellow vertical tail surfaces with a blue flash superimposed; white code 'S' on fin, repeated on blue nose wheel door. Blue wingtips

Hawker Hunter F. Mk.1, WW636/Q, flown by 'B' Flight Commander, No 54 Squadron RAF, Odiham, 1955. Dark Sea Grey BS 638/Dark Green BS 641 upper surfaces with Aluminium undersides; blue/yellow checks flanking unit marking on nose. Black serial repeated below wings; yellow 'Q' on fin, repeated on blue nose wheel door together with the squadron marking also in yellow. Blue fin with yellow flash; blue wingtips

Hawker Hunter F. Mk.1, WT617/D, Day Fighter Leader School, Central Fighter Establishment RAF, West Raynham, 1956. Dark Sea Grey BS 638/Dark Green BS 641 upper surfaces with Aluminium undersides; yellow trim to dorsal spine and fin leading edge. Black serial, repeated below wings; white code 'D' on rear fuselage

Hawker Hunter *F. Mk.1, WW604/F, No 233 Operational Conversion Unit RAF, Pembry, 1957. Dark Sea Grey BS 638/Dark Green BS 641 upper surfaces with Aluminium undersides; yellow wingtips and code 'F' on rear fuselage. Black serial repeated below wings*

Hawker Hunter *F. Mk. 2, WN949/R, No 257 Squadron RAF, Wattisham, 1955. Dark Sea Grey BS 638/Dark Green BS 641 upper surfaces with Aluminium undersides; yellow/mid-green checks flanking fuselage roundels. Black serial, repeated below wings; yellow code 'R' on fin, outlined in mid-green, repeated in green on yellow nose wheel door*

Hawker Hunter *F. Mk. 2, WN907/H, No 257 Squadron RAF, Wattisham, 1956. Dark Sea Grey BS 638/Dark Green BS 641 upper surfaces with Aluminium undersides; yellow/mid-green checks flanking unit marking on nose. Black serial, repeated below wings; yellow code 'H' on fin, outlined in mid-green, repeated in mid-green on yellow nose wheel door*

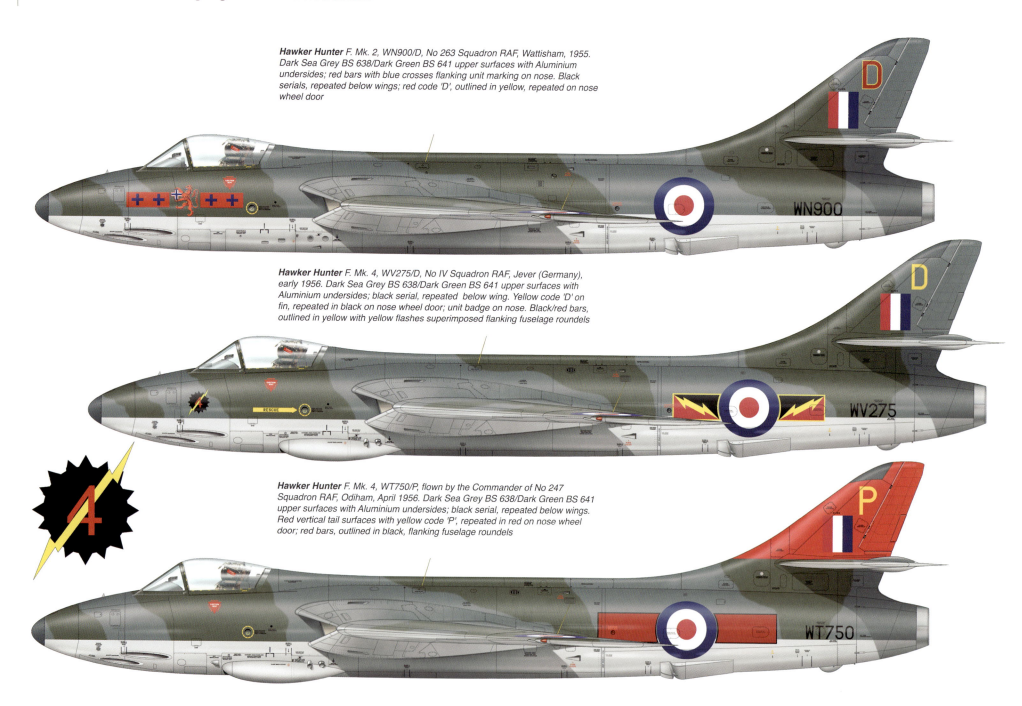

Hawker Hunter *F. Mk. 2, WN900/D, No 263 Squadron RAF, Wattisham, 1955. Dark Sea Grey BS 638/Dark Green BS 641 upper surfaces with Aluminium undersides; red bars with blue crosses flanking unit marking on nose. Black serials, repeated below wings; red code 'D', outlined in yellow, repeated on nose wheel door*

Hawker Hunter *F. Mk. 4, WV275/D, No IV Squadron RAF, Jever (Germany), early 1956. Dark Sea Grey BS 638/Dark Green BS 641 upper surfaces with Aluminium undersides; black serial, repeated below wing. Yellow code 'D' on fin, repeated in black on nose wheel door; unit badge on nose. Black/red bars, outlined in yellow with yellow flashes superimposed flanking fuselage roundels*

Hawker Hunter *F. Mk. 4, WT750/P, flown by the Commander of No 247 Squadron RAF, Odiham, April 1956. Dark Sea Grey BS 638/Dark Green BS 641 upper surfaces with Aluminium undersides; black serial, repeated below wings. Red vertical tail surfaces with yellow code 'P', repeated in red on nose wheel door; red bars, outlined in black, flanking fuselage roundels*

Hawker Hunter F. Mk. 4, WT743/R, No 118 Squadron RAF, Jever (Germany), 1956. Dark Sea Grey BS 638/Dark Green BS 641 upper surfaces with Aluminium undersides; black serial, repeated below wings. Yellow code 'R' on fin, repeated in black on nose wheel door; black/white 'waves' flanking fuselage roundels, repeated on nose flanking unit crest

Hawker Hunter F. Mk. 4, WV314/B, No 92 Squadron RAF, Linton-on-Ouse, early 1957. Dark Sea Grey BS 638/Dark Green BS 641 upper surfaces with Aluminium undersides; black serials, repeated below wings. Light Grey code 'B' on fin, repeated in black on nose wheel door; yellow/red checks flanking unit marking on nose

Hawker Hunter F. Mk. 4, WV330/D, No 245 Squadron RAF, Stradishall, July 1957. Dark Sea Grey BS 638/Dark Green BS 641 upper surfaces with Aluminium undersides; black serials, repeated below wings. Yellow code 'D' on fin, repeated in black on nose wheel door; mid-blue/yellow checks on nose

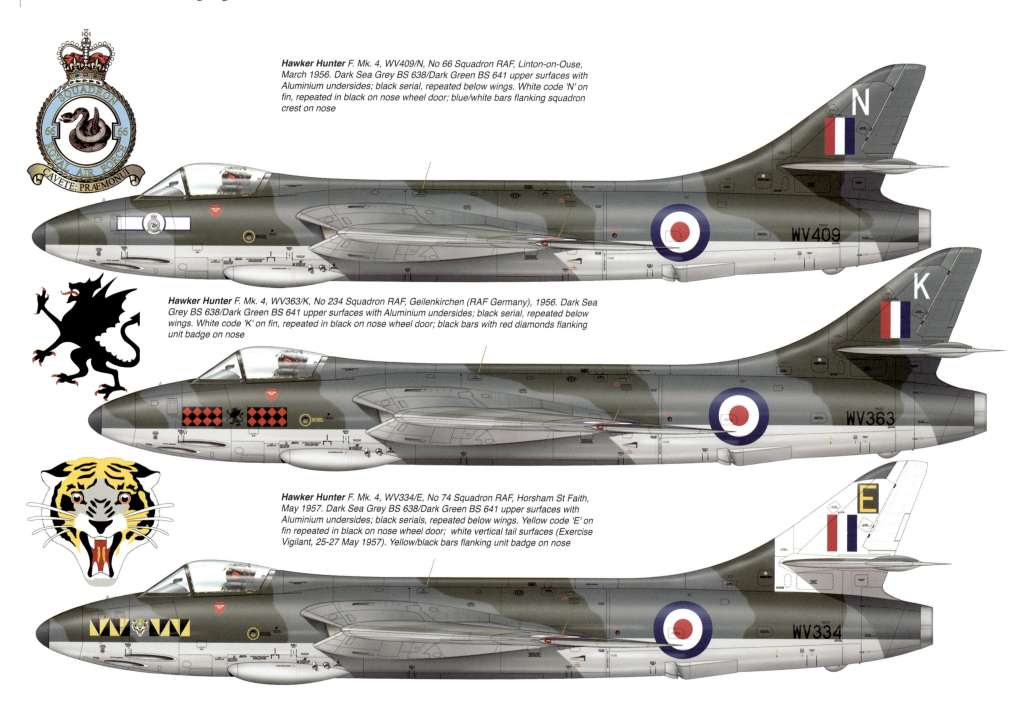

Hawker Hunter *F. Mk. 4, WV409/N, No 66 Squadron RAF, Linton-on-Ouse, March 1956. Dark Sea Grey BS 638/Dark Green BS 641 upper surfaces with Aluminium undersides; black serial, repeated below wings. White code 'N' on fin, repeated in black on nose wheel door; blue/white bars flanking squadron crest on nose*

Hawker Hunter *F. Mk. 4, WV363/K, No 234 Squadron RAF, Geilenkirchen (RAF Germany), 1956. Dark Sea Grey BS 638/Dark Green BS 641 upper surfaces with Aluminium undersides; black serial, repeated below wings. White code 'K' on fin, repeated in black on nose wheel door; black bars with red diamonds flanking unit badge on nose*

Hawker Hunter *F. Mk. 4, WV334/E, No 74 Squadron RAF, Horsham St Faith, May 1957. Dark Sea Grey BS 638/Dark Green BS 641 upper surfaces with Aluminium undersides; black serials, repeated below wings. Yellow code 'E' on fin repeated in black on nose wheel door; white vertical tail surfaces (Exercise Vigilant, 25-27 May 1957). Yellow/black bars flanking unit badge on nose*

Hawker Hunter *F. Mk. 4, WT802/P, No 98 Squadron, RAF Jever (Germany), 1956. Dark Sea Grey BS 638/Dark Green BS 641 upper surfaces with Aluminium undersides; black serial repeated below wings. White code letter, repeated on red nosewheel door; red/white bars flanking fuselage roundels, repeated on nose flanking unit crest*

Hawker Hunter *F. Mk. 4, WV399/B, No 222 Squadron, RAF Leuchars, 1957. Dark Sea Grey BS 638/Dark Green BS 641 upper surfaces with Aluminium undersides; black serial, repeated below wings. White code 'B' on fin, repeated in black on nosewheel door; blue/red checks flanking fuselage roundels*

Hawker Hunter *F. Mk. 4, WV379/V, No 111 Squadron, RAF, North Weald, 1956. Dark Sea Grey BS 638/Dark Green BS 641 upper surfaces with Aluminium undersides; black serials, repeated below wings. Black code 'V', outlined in yellow, repeated on nosewheel door; black/yellow bars flanking fuselage roundel. Red wingtips, unit crest on nose*

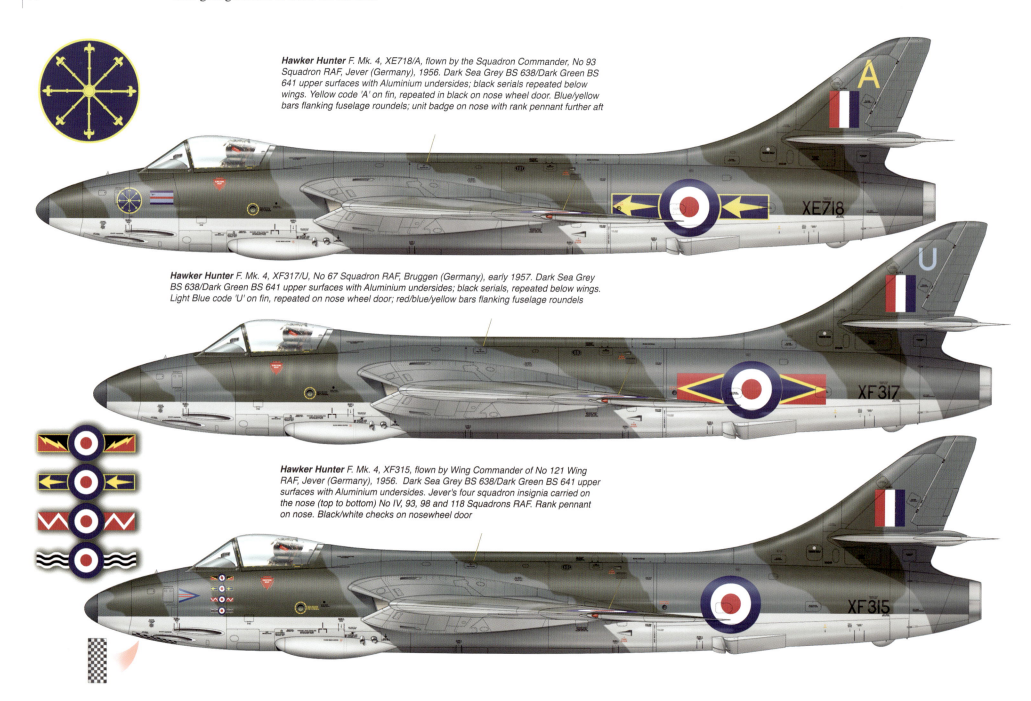

Hawker Hunter F. Mk. 4, XE718/A, flown by the Squadron Commander, No 93 Squadron RAF, Jever (Germany), 1956. Dark Sea Grey BS 638/Dark Green BS 641 upper surfaces with Aluminium undersides; black serials repeated below wings. Yellow code 'A' on fin, repeated in black on nose wheel door. Blue/yellow bars flanking fuselage roundels; unit badge on nose with rank pennant further aft

Hawker Hunter F. Mk. 4, XF317/U, No 67 Squadron RAF, Bruggen (Germany), early 1957. Dark Sea Grey BS 638/Dark Green BS 641 upper surfaces with Aluminium undersides; black serials, repeated below wings. Light Blue code 'U' on fin, repeated on nose wheel door; red/blue/yellow bars flanking fuselage roundels

Hawker Hunter F. Mk. 4, XF315, flown by Wing Commander of No 121 Wing RAF, Jever (Germany), 1956. Dark Sea Grey BS 638/Dark Green BS 641 upper surfaces with Aluminium undersides. Jever's four squadron insignia carried on the nose (top to bottom) No IV, 93, 98 and 118 Squadrons RAF. Rank pennant on nose. Black/white checks on nosewheel door

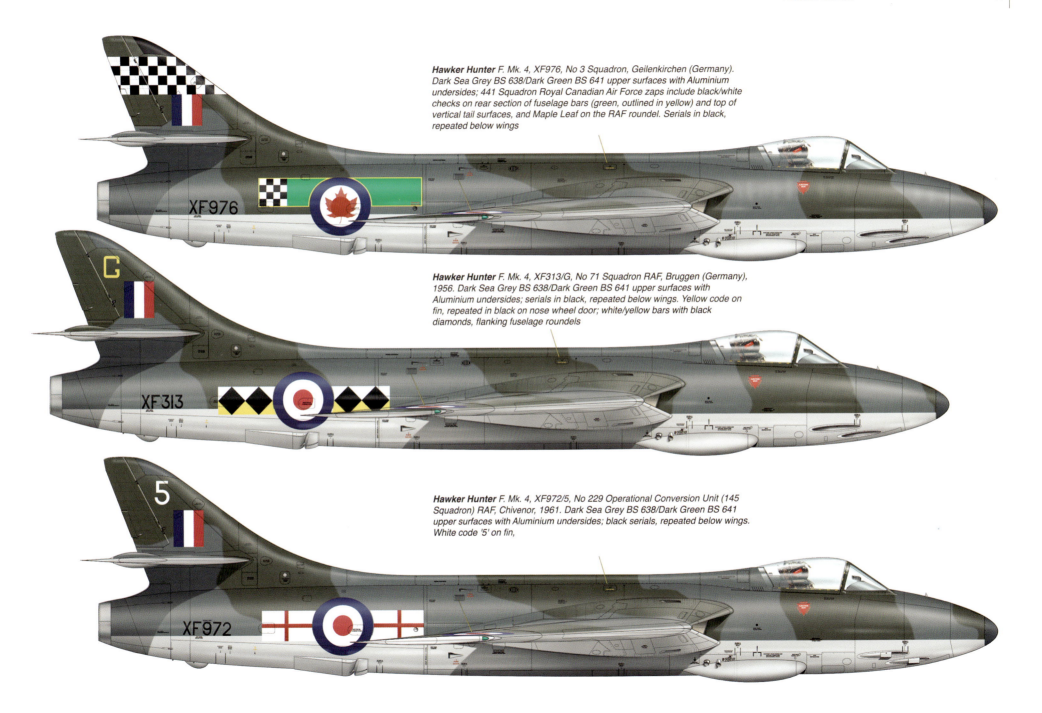

Hawker Hunter *F. Mk. 4, XF976, No 3 Squadron, Geilenkirchen (Germany). Dark Sea Grey BS 638/Dark Green BS 641 upper surfaces with Aluminium undersides; 441 Squadron Royal Canadian Air Force zaps include black/white checks on rear section of fuselage bars (green, outlined in yellow) and top of vertical tail surfaces, and Maple Leaf on the RAF roundel. Serials in black, repeated below wings*

Hawker Hunter *F. Mk. 4, XF313/G, No 71 Squadron RAF, Bruggen (Germany), 1956. Dark Sea Grey BS 638/Dark Green BS 641 upper surfaces with Aluminium undersides; serials in black, repeated below wings. Yellow code on fin, repeated in black on nose wheel door; white/yellow bars with black diamonds, flanking fuselage roundels*

Hawker Hunter *F. Mk. 4, XF972/5, No 229 Operational Conversion Unit (145 Squadron) RAF, Chivenor, 1961. Dark Sea Grey BS 638/Dark Green BS 641 upper surfaces with Aluminium undersides; black serials, repeated below wings. White code '5' on fin,*

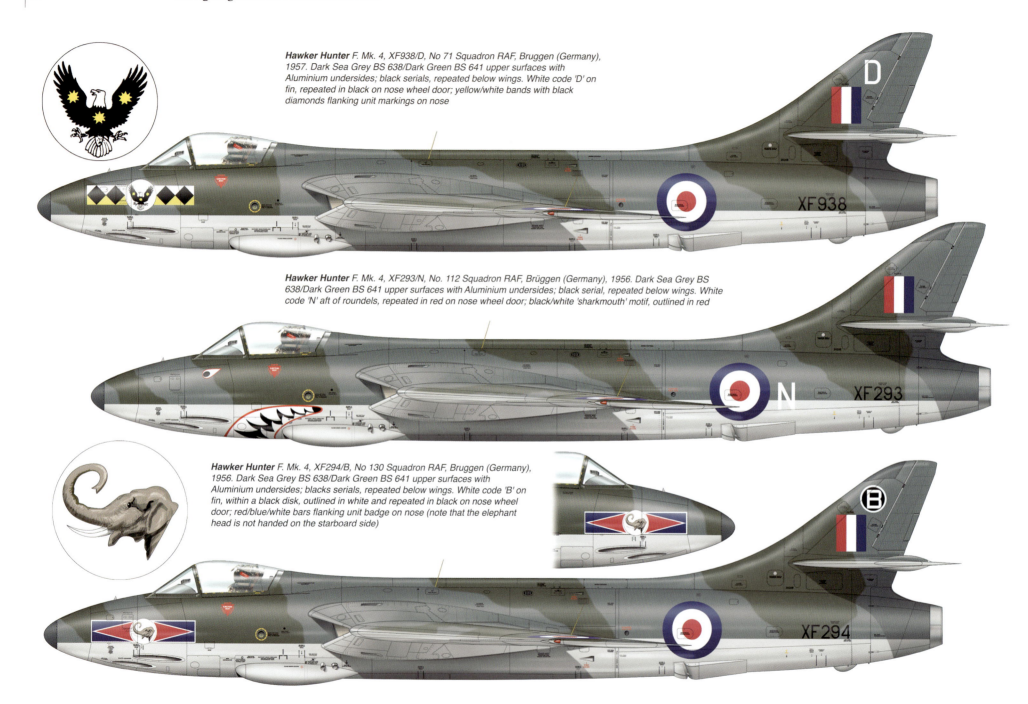

Hawker Hunter F. Mk. 4, XF938/D, No 71 Squadron RAF, Bruggen (Germany), 1957. Dark Sea Grey BS 638/Dark Green BS 641 upper surfaces with Aluminium undersides; black serials, repeated below wings. White code 'D' on fin, repeated in black on nose wheel door; yellow/white bands with black diamonds flanking unit markings on nose

Hawker Hunter F. Mk. 4, XF293/N, No. 112 Squadron RAF, Brüggen (Germany), 1956. Dark Sea Grey BS 638/Dark Green BS 641 upper surfaces with Aluminium undersides; black serial, repeated below wings. White code 'N' aft of roundels, repeated in red on nose wheel door; black/white 'sharkmouth' motif, outlined in red

Hawker Hunter F. Mk. 4, XF294/B, No 130 Squadron RAF, Bruggen (Germany), 1956. Dark Sea Grey BS 638/Dark Green BS 641 upper surfaces with Aluminium undersides; blacks serials, repeated below wings. White code 'B' on fin, within a black disk, outlined in white and repeated in black on nose wheel door; red/blue/white bars flanking unit badge on nose (note that the elephant head is not handed on the starboard side)

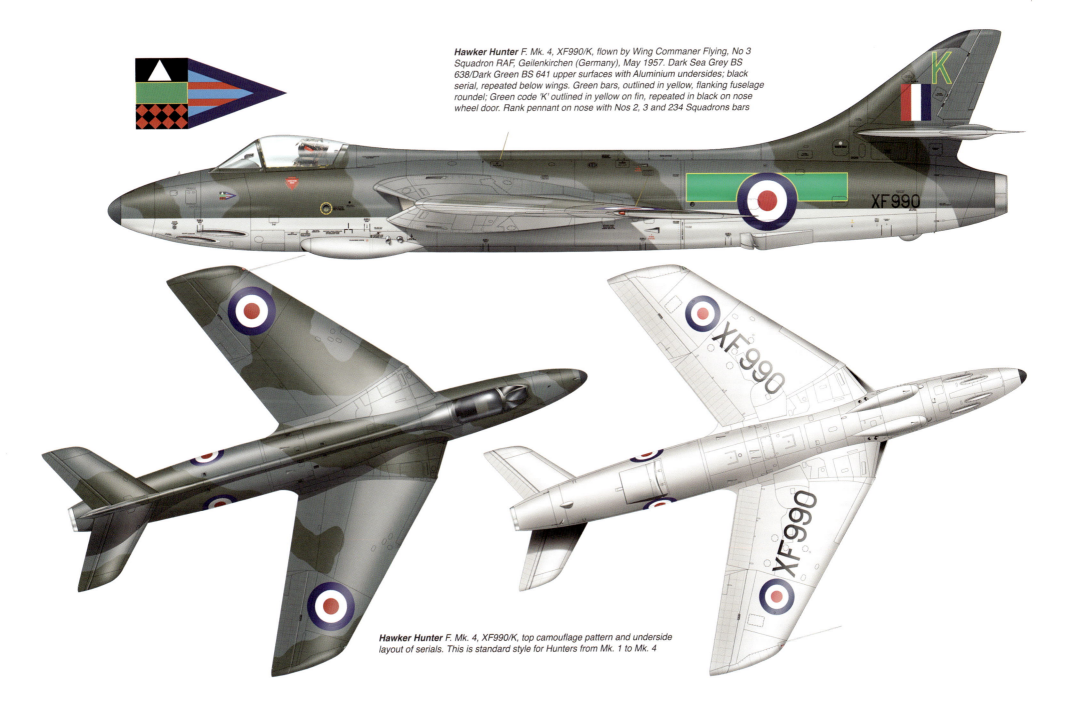

Hawker Hunter F. Mk. 4, XF990/K, flown by Wing Commaner Flying, No 3 Squadron RAF, Geilenkirchen (Germany), May 1957. Dark Sea Grey BS 638/Dark Green BS 641 upper surfaces with Aluminium undersides; black serial, repeated below wings. Green bars, outlined in yellow, flanking fuselage roundel; Green code 'K' outlined in yellow on fin, repeated in black on nose wheel door. Rank pennant on nose with Nos 2, 3 and 234 Squadrons bars

Hawker Hunter F. Mk. 4, XF990/K, top camouflage pattern and underside layout of serials. This is standard style for Hunters from Mk. 1 to Mk. 4

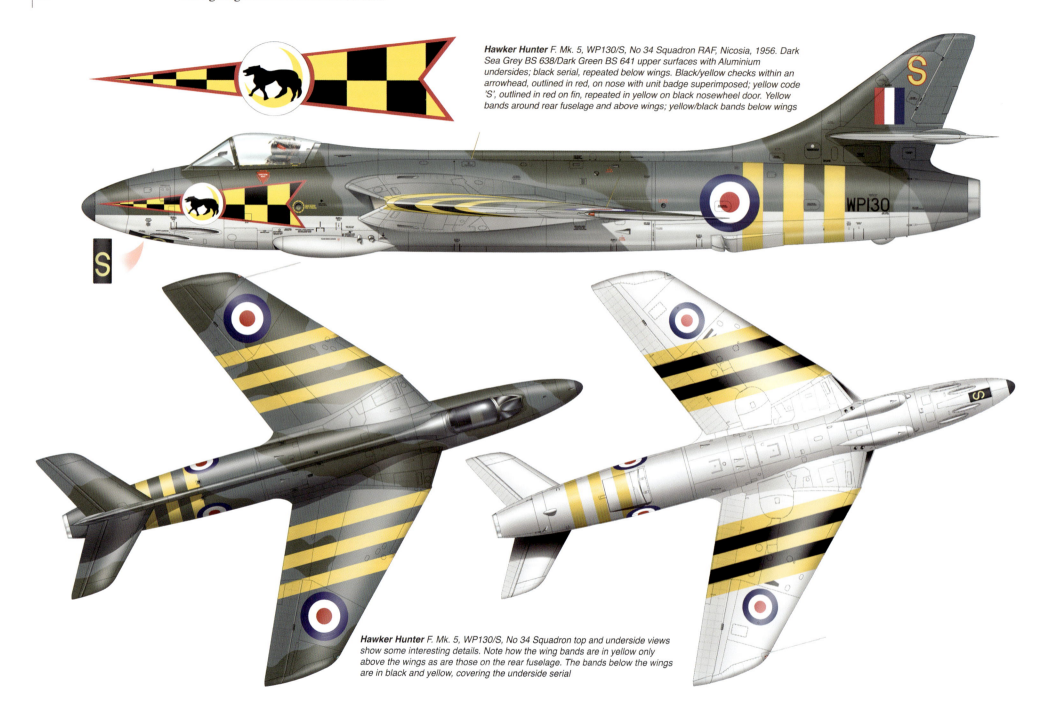

Hawker Hunter F. Mk. 5, WP130/S, No 34 Squadron RAF, Nicosia, 1956. Dark Sea Grey BS 638/Dark Green BS 641 upper surfaces with Aluminium undersides; black serial, repeated below wings. Black/yellow checks within an arrowhead, outlined in red, on nose with unit badge superimposed; yellow code 'S', outlined in red on fin, repeated in yellow on black nosewheel door. Yellow bands around rear fuselage and above wings; yellow/black bands below wings

Hawker Hunter F. Mk. 5, WP130/S, No 34 Squadron top and underside views show some interesting details. Note how the wing bands are in yellow only above the wings as are those on the rear fuselage. The bands below the wings are in black and yellow, covering the underside serial

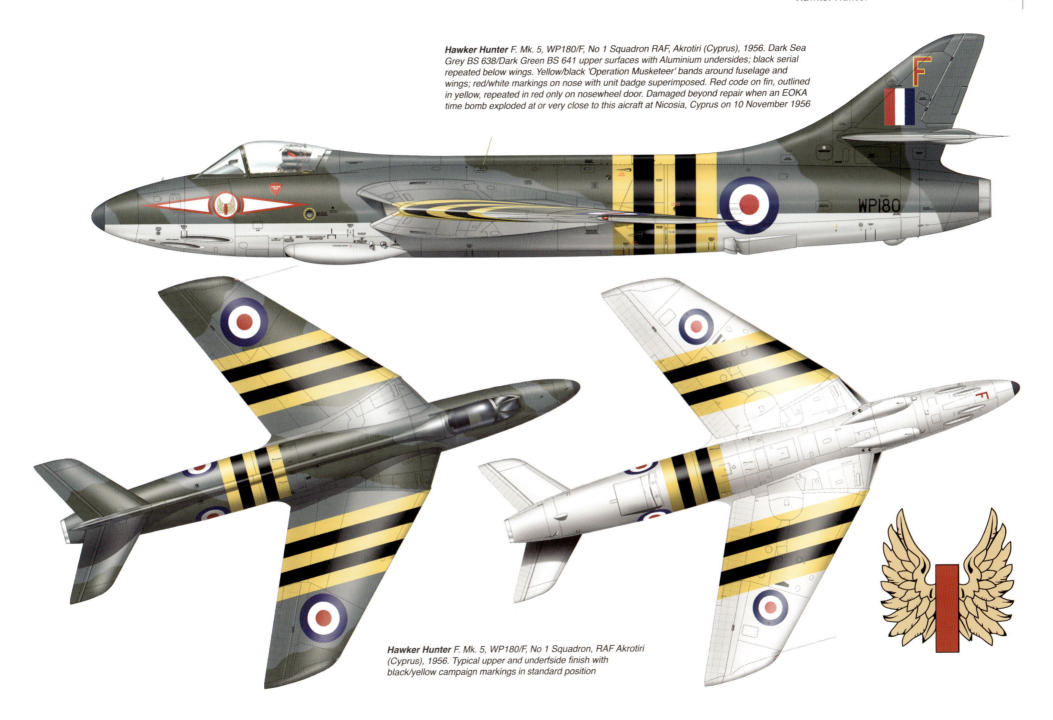

Hawker Hunter *F. Mk. 5, WP180/F, No 1 Squadron RAF, Akrotiri (Cyprus), 1956. Dark Sea Grey BS 638/Dark Green BS 641 upper surfaces with Aluminium undersides; black serial repeated below wings. Yellow/black 'Operation Musketeer' bands around fuselage and wings; red/white markings on nose with unit badge superimposed. Red code on fin, outlined in yellow, repeated in red only on nosewheel door. Damaged beyond repair when an EOKA time bomb exploded at or very close to this aicraft at Nicosia, Cyprus on 10 November 1956*

Hawker Hunter *F. Mk. 5, WP180/F, No 1 Squadron, RAF Akrotiri (Cyprus), 1956. Typical upper and underfside finish with black/yellow campaign markings in standard position*

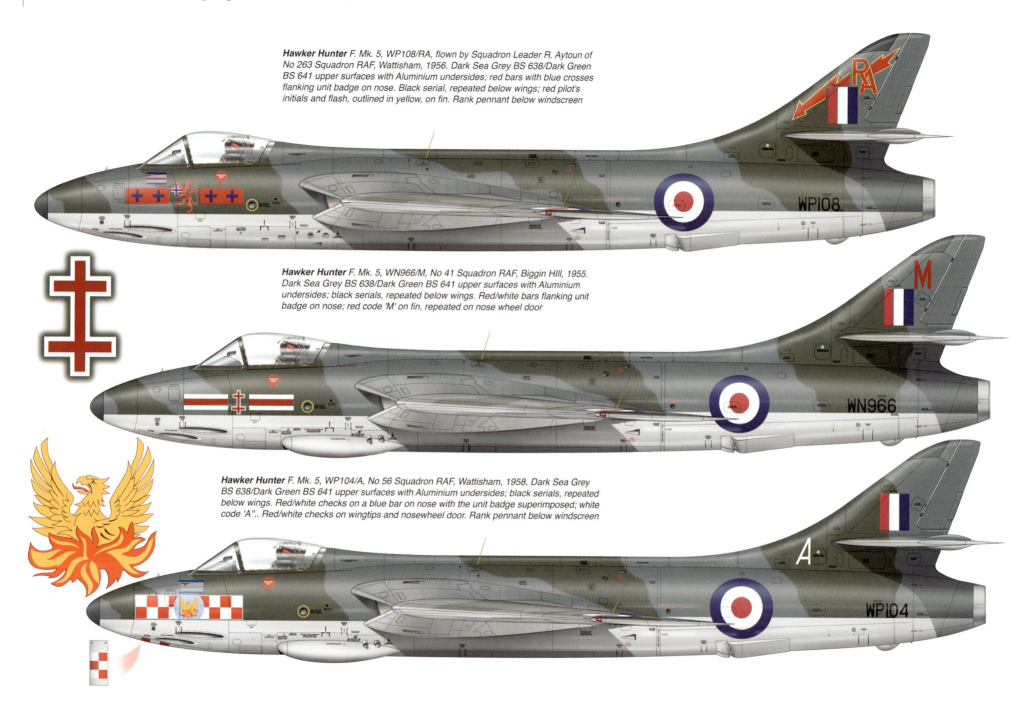

Hawker Hunter F. Mk. 5, WP108/RA, flown by Squadron Leader R. Aytoun of No 263 Squadron RAF, Wattisham, 1956. Dark Sea Grey BS 638/Dark Green BS 641 upper surfaces with Aluminium undersides; red bars with blue crosses flanking unit badge on nose. Black serial, repeated below wings; red pilot's initials and flash, outlined in yellow, on fin. Rank pennant below windscreen

Hawker Hunter F. Mk. 5, WN966/M, No 41 Squadron RAF, Biggin HIll, 1955. Dark Sea Grey BS 638/Dark Green BS 641 upper surfaces with Aluminium undersides; black serials, repeated below wings. Red/white bars flanking unit badge on nose; red code 'M' on fin, repeated on nose wheel door

Hawker Hunter F. Mk. 5, WP104/A, No 56 Squadron RAF, Wattisham, 1958. Dark Sea Grey BS 638/Dark Green BS 641 upper surfaces with Aluminium undersides; black serials, repeated below wings. Red/white checks on a blue bar on nose with the unit badge superimposed; white code 'A''.. Red/white checks on wingtips and nosewheel door. Rank pennant below windscreen

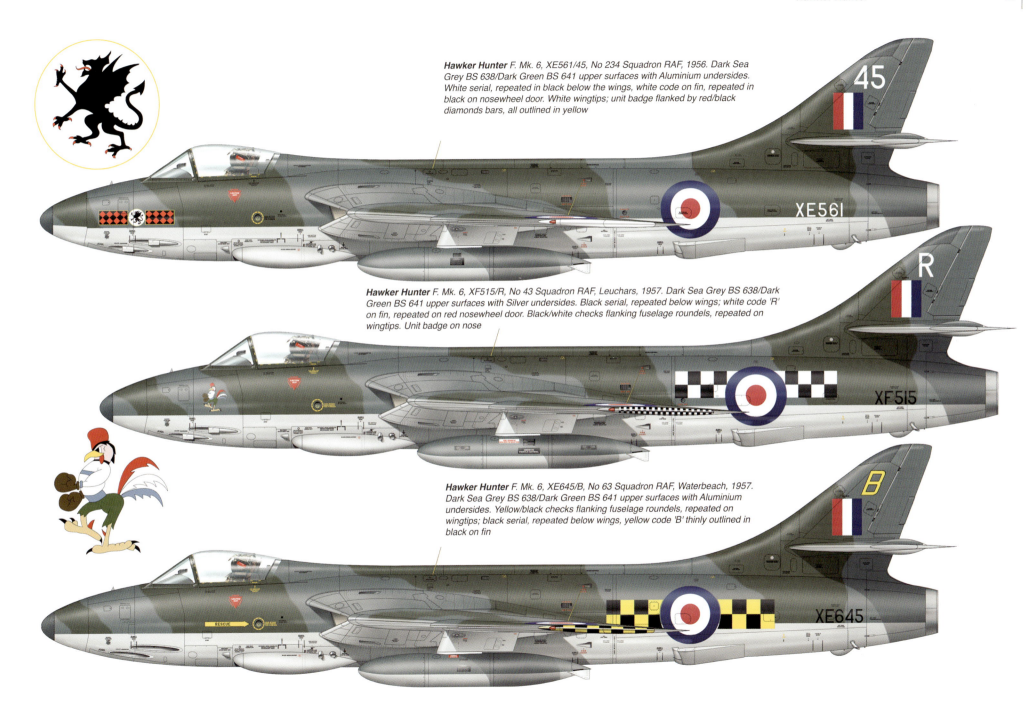

Hawker Hunter *F. Mk. 6, XE561/45, No 234 Squadron RAF, 1956. Dark Sea Grey BS 638/Dark Green BS 641 upper surfaces with Aluminium undersides. White serial, repeated in black below the wings, white code on fin, repeated in black on nosewheel door. White wingtips; unit badge flanked by red/black diamonds bars, all outlined in yellow*

Hawker Hunter *F. Mk. 6, XF515/R, No 43 Squadron RAF, Leuchars, 1957. Dark Sea Grey BS 638/Dark Green BS 641 upper surfaces with Silver undersides. Black serial, repeated below wings; white code 'R' on fin, repeated on red nosewheel door. Black/white checks flanking fuselage roundels, repeated on wingtips. Unit badge on nose*

Hawker Hunter *F. Mk. 6, XE645/B, No 63 Squadron RAF, Waterbeach, 1957. Dark Sea Grey BS 638/Dark Green BS 641 upper surfaces with Aluminium undersides. Yellow/black checks flanking fuselage roundels, repeated on wingtips; black serial, repeated below wings, yellow code 'B' thinly outlined in black on fin*

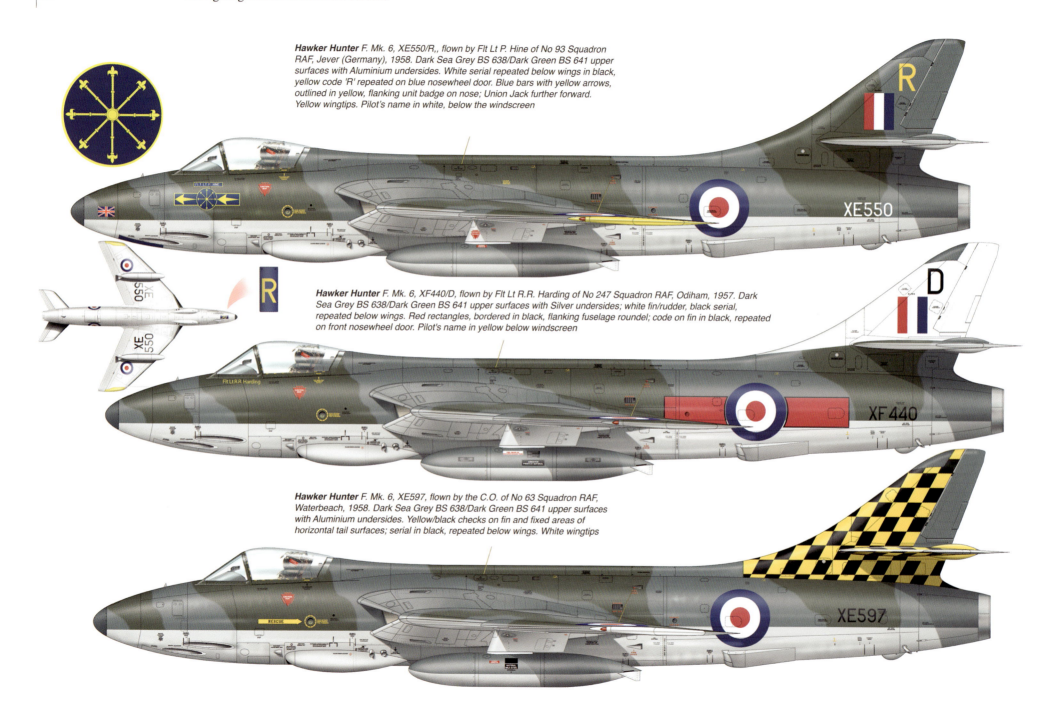

Hawker Hunter *F. Mk. 6, XE550/R,, flown by Flt Lt P. Hine of No 93 Squadron RAF, Jever (Germany), 1958. Dark Sea Grey BS 638/Dark Green BS 641 upper surfaces with Aluminium undersides. White serial repeated below wings in black, yellow code 'R' repeated on blue nosewheel door. Blue bars with yellow arrows, outlined in yellow, flanking unit badge on nose; Union Jack further forward. Yellow wingtips. Pilot's name in white, below the windscreen*

Hawker Hunter *F. Mk. 6, XF440/D, flown by Flt Lt R.R. Harding of No 247 Squadron RAF, Odiham, 1957. Dark Sea Grey BS 638/Dark Green BS 641 upper surfaces with Silver undersides; white fin/rudder, black serial, repeated below wings. Red rectangles, bordered in black, flanking fuselage roundel; code on fin in black, repeated on front nosewheel door. Pilot's name in yellow below windscreen*

Hawker Hunter *F. Mk. 6, XE597, flown by the C.O. of No 63 Squadron RAF, Waterbeach, 1958. Dark Sea Grey BS 638/Dark Green BS 641 upper surfaces with Aluminium undersides. Yellow/black checks on fin and fixed areas of horizontal tail surfaces; serial in black, repeated below wings. White wingtips*

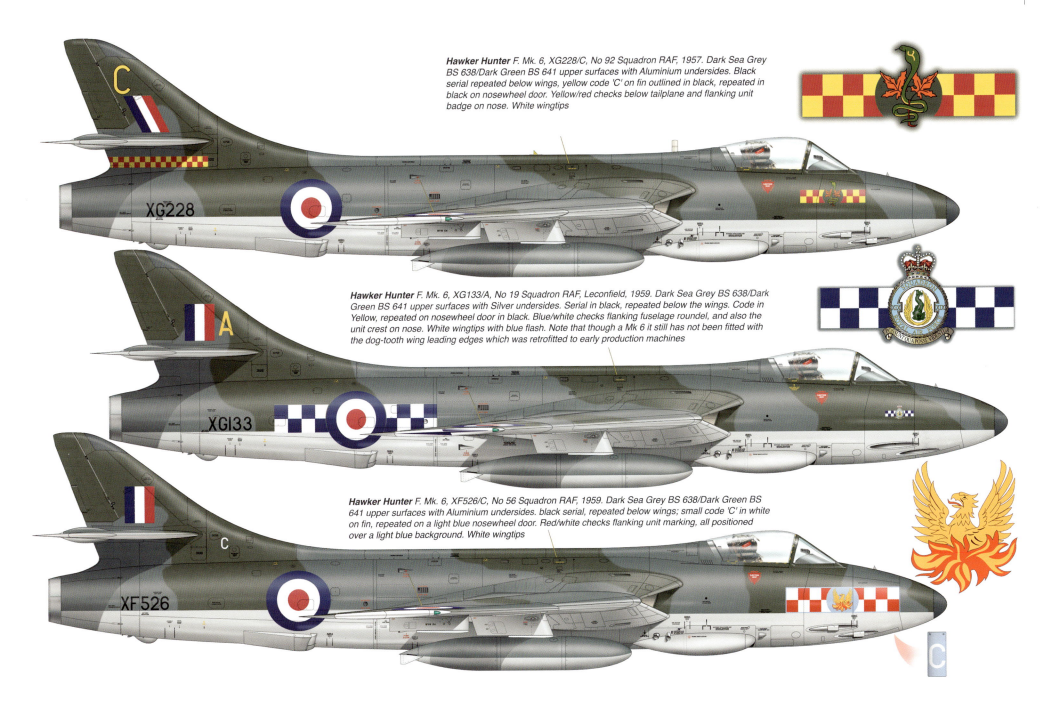

Hawker Hunter F. Mk. 6, XG228/C, No 92 Squadron RAF, 1957. Dark Sea Grey BS 638/Dark Green BS 641 upper surfaces with Aluminium undersides. Black serial repeated below wings, yellow code 'C' on fin outlined in black, repeated in black on nosewheel door. Yellow/red checks below tailplane and flanking unit badge on nose. White wingtips

Hawker Hunter F. Mk. 6, XG133/A, No 19 Squadron RAF, Leconfield, 1959. Dark Sea Grey BS 638/Dark Green BS 641 upper surfaces with Silver undersides. Serial in black, repeated below the wings. Code in Yellow, repeated on nosewheel door in black. Blue/white checks flanking fuselage roundel, and also the unit crest on nose. White wingtips with blue flash. Note that though a Mk 6 it still has not been fitted with the dog-tooth wing leading edges which was retrofitted to early production machines

Hawker Hunter F. Mk. 6, XF526/C, No 56 Squadron RAF, 1959. Dark Sea Grey BS 638/Dark Green BS 641 upper surfaces with Aluminium undersides. black serial, repeated below wings; small code 'C' in white on fin, repeated on a light blue nosewheel door. Red/white checks flanking unit marking, all positioned over a light blue background. White wingtips

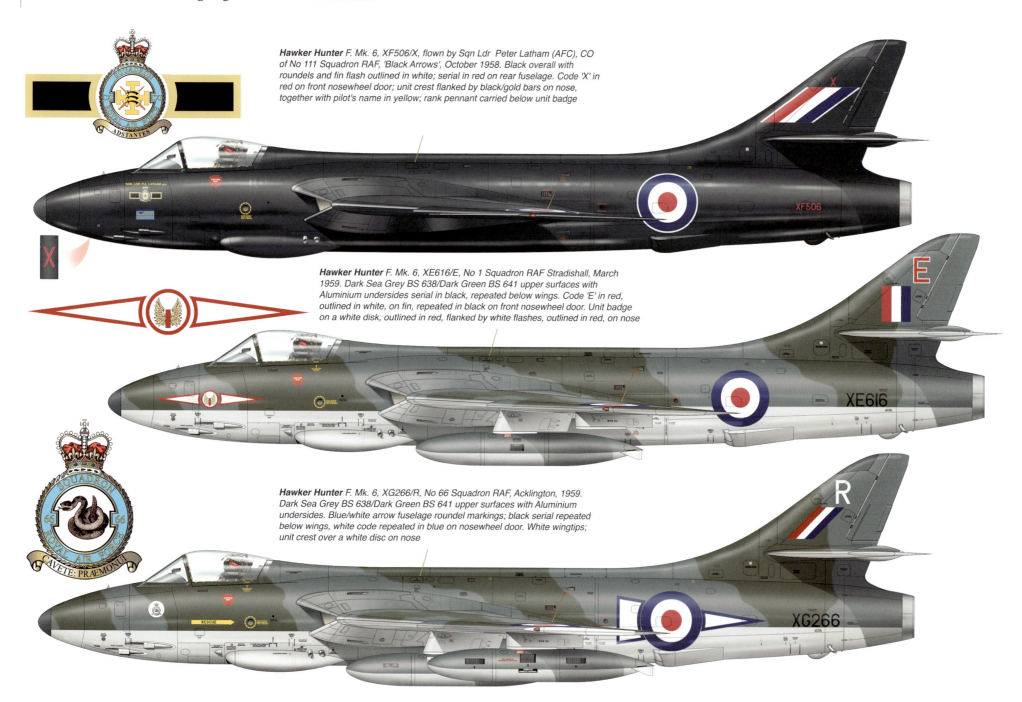

Hawker Hunter F. Mk. 6, XF506/X, flown by Sqn Ldr Peter Latham (AFC), CO of No 111 Squadron RAF, 'Black Arrows', October 1958. Black overall with roundels and fin flash outlined in white; serial in red on rear fuselage. Code 'X' in red on front nosewheel door; unit crest flanked by black/gold bars on nose, together with pilot's name in yellow; rank pennant carried below unit badge

Hawker Hunter F. Mk. 6, XE616/E, No 1 Squadron RAF Stradishall, March 1959. Dark Sea Grey BS 638/Dark Green BS 641 upper surfaces with Aluminium undersides serial in black, repeated below wings. Code 'E' in red, outlined in white, on fin, repeated in black on front nosewheel door. Unit badge on a white disk, outlined in red, flanked by white flashes, outlined in red, on nose

Hawker Hunter F. Mk. 6, XG266/R, No 66 Squadron RAF, Acklington, 1959. Dark Sea Grey BS 638/Dark Green BS 641 upper surfaces with Aluminium undersides. Blue/white arrow fuselage roundel markings; black serial repeated below wings, white code repeated in blue on nosewheel door. White wingtips; unit crest over a white disc on nose

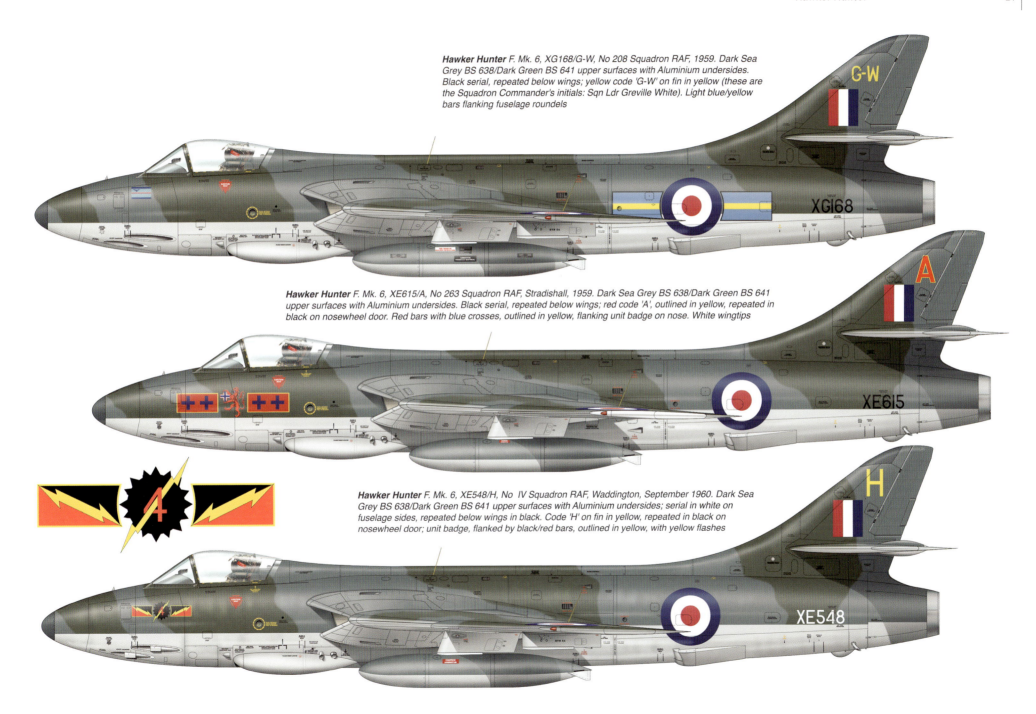

Hawker Hunter F. Mk. 6, XG168/G-W, No 208 Squadron RAF, 1959. Dark Sea Grey BS 638/Dark Green BS 641 upper surfaces with Aluminium undersides. Black serial, repeated below wings; yellow code 'G-W' on fin in yellow (these are the Squadron Commander's initials: Sqn Ldr Greville White). Light blue/yellow bars flanking fuselage roundels

Hawker Hunter F. Mk. 6, XE615/A, No 263 Squadron RAF, Stradishall, 1959. Dark Sea Grey BS 638/Dark Green BS 641 upper surfaces with Aluminium undersides. Black serial, repeated below wings; red code 'A', outlined in yellow, repeated in black on nosewheel door. Red bars with blue crosses, outlined in yellow, flanking unit badge on nose. White wingtips

Hawker Hunter F. Mk. 6, XE548/H, No IV Squadron RAF, Waddington, September 1960. Dark Sea Grey BS 638/Dark Green BS 641 upper surfaces with Aluminium undersides; serial in white on fuselage sides, repeated below wings in black. Code 'H' on fin in yellow, repeated in black on nosewheel door; unit badge, flanked by black/red bars, outlined in yellow, with yellow flashes

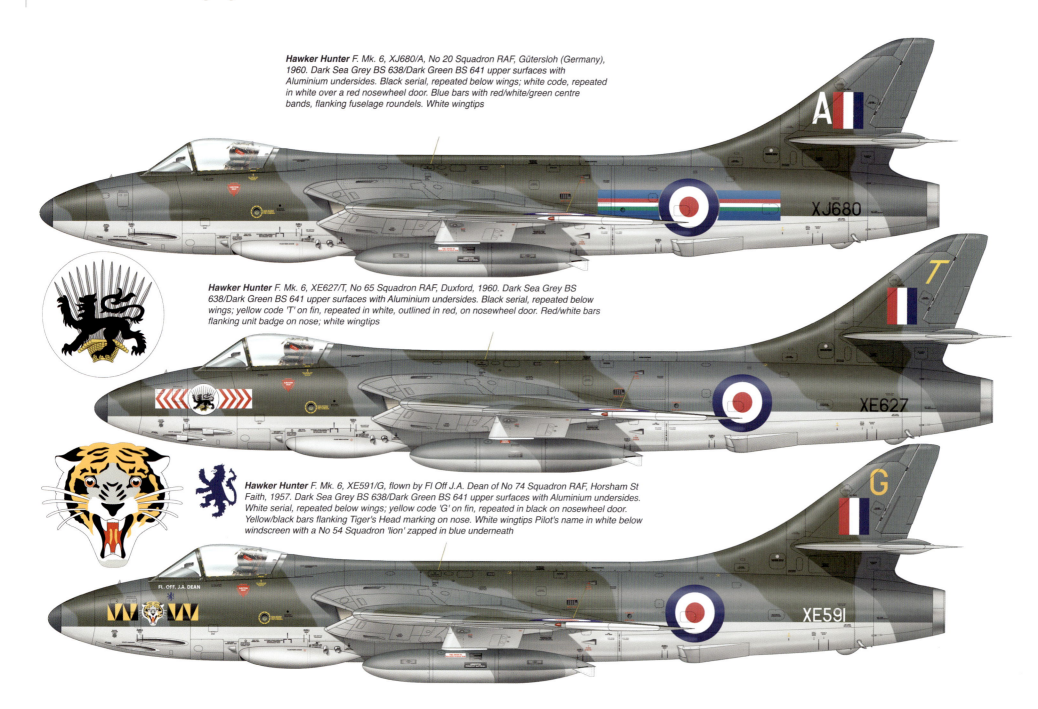

Hawker Hunter F. Mk. 6, XJ680/A, No 20 Squadron RAF, Gütersloh (Germany), 1960. Dark Sea Grey BS 638/Dark Green BS 641 upper surfaces with Aluminium undersides. Black serial, repeated below wings; white code, repeated in white over a red nosewheel door. Blue bars with red/white/green centre bands, flanking fuselage roundels. White wingtips

Hawker Hunter F. Mk. 6, XE627/T, No 65 Squadron RAF, Duxford, 1960. Dark Sea Grey BS 638/Dark Green BS 641 upper surfaces with Aluminium undersides. Black serial, repeated below wings; yellow code 'T' on fin, repeated in white, outlined in red, on nosewheel door. Red/white bars flanking unit badge on nose; white wingtips

Hawker Hunter F. Mk. 6, XE591/G, flown by Fl Off J.A. Dean of No 74 Squadron RAF, Horsham St Faith, 1957. Dark Sea Grey BS 638/Dark Green BS 641 upper surfaces with Aluminium undersides. White serial, repeated below wings; yellow code 'G' on fin, repeated in black on nosewheel door. Yellow/black bars flanking Tiger's Head marking on nose. White wingtips Pilot's name in white below windscreen with a No 54 Squadron 'lion' zapped in blue underneath

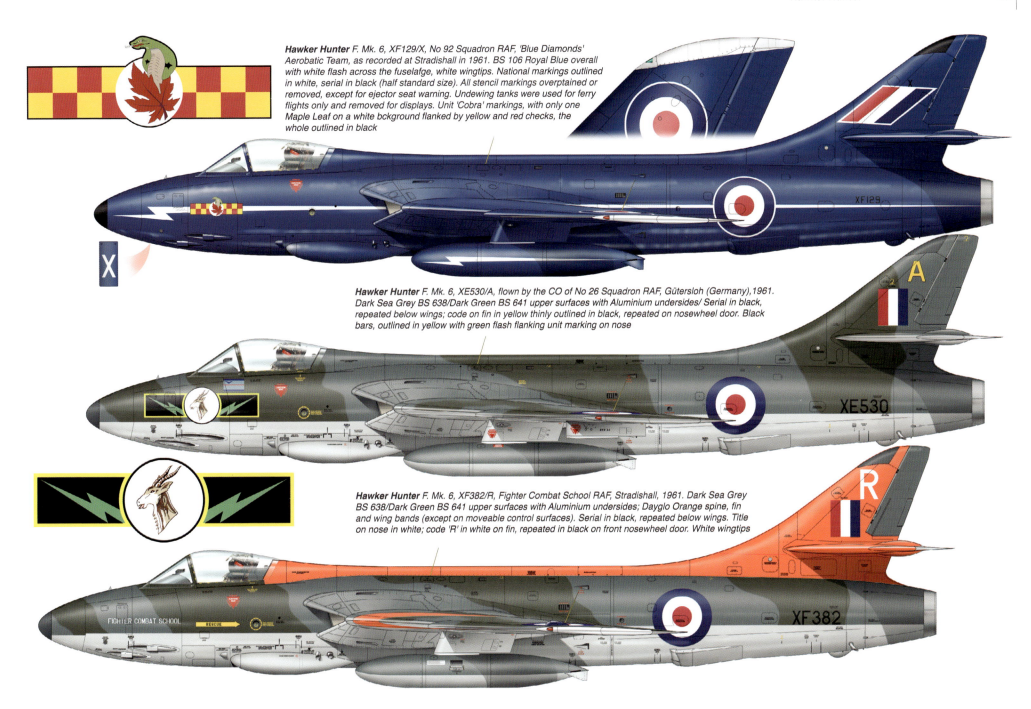

Hawker Hunter F. Mk. 6, XF129/X, No 92 Squadron RAF, 'Blue Diamonds' Aerobatic Team, as recorded at Stradishall in 1961. BS 106 Royal Blue overall with white flash across the fuselafge, white wingtips. National markings outlined in white, serial in black (half standard size). All stencil markings overptained or removed, except for ejector seat warning. Undewing tanks were used for ferry flights only and removed for displays. Unit 'Cobra' markings, with only one Maple Leaf on a white bckground flanked by yellow and red checks, the whole outlined in black

Hawker Hunter F. Mk. 6, XE530/A, flown by the CO of No 26 Squadron RAF, Gütersloh (Germany),1961. Dark Sea Grey BS 638/Dark Green BS 641 upper surfaces with Aluminium undersides/ Serial in black, repeated below wings; code on fin in yellow thinly outlined in black, repeated on nosewheel door. Black bars, outlined in yellow with green flash flanking unit marking on nose

Hawker Hunter F. Mk. 6, XF382/R, Fighter Combat School RAF, Stradishall, 1961. Dark Sea Grey BS 638/Dark Green BS 641 upper surfaces with Aluminium undersides; Dayglo Orange spine, fin and wing bands (except on moveable control surfaces). Serial in black, repeated below wings. Title on nose in white; code 'R' in white on fin, repeated in black on front nosewheel door. White wingtips

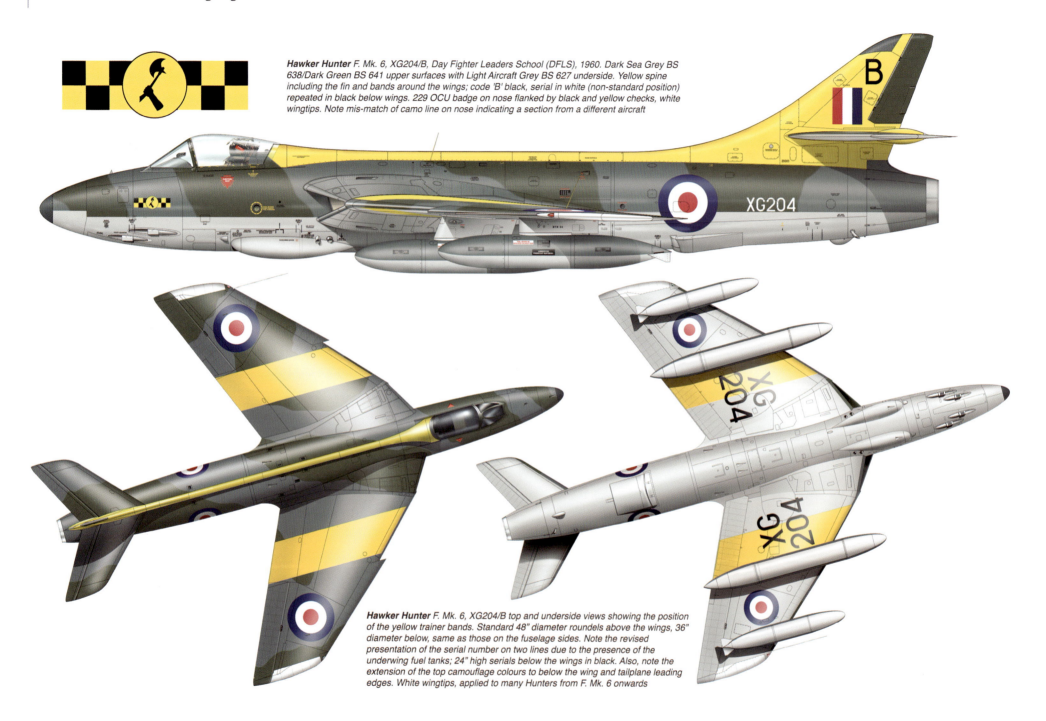

Hawker Hunter F. Mk. 6, XG204/B, Day Fighter Leaders School (DFLS), 1960. Dark Sea Grey BS 638/Dark Green BS 641 upper surfaces with Light Aircraft Grey BS 627 underside. Yellow spine including the fin and bands around the wings; code 'B' black, serial in white (non-standard position) repeated in black below wings. 229 OCU badge on nose flanked by black and yellow checks, white wingtips. Note mis-match of camo line on nose indicating a section from a different aircraft

Hawker Hunter F. Mk. 6, XG204/B top and underside views showing the position of the yellow trainer bands. Standard 48" diameter roundels above the wings, 36" diameter below, same as those on the fuselage sides. Note the revised presentation of the serial number on two lines due to the presence of the underwing fuel tanks; 24" high serials below the wings in black. Also, note the extension of the top camouflage colours to below the wing and tailplane leading edges. White wingtips, applied to many Hunters from F. Mk. 6 onwards

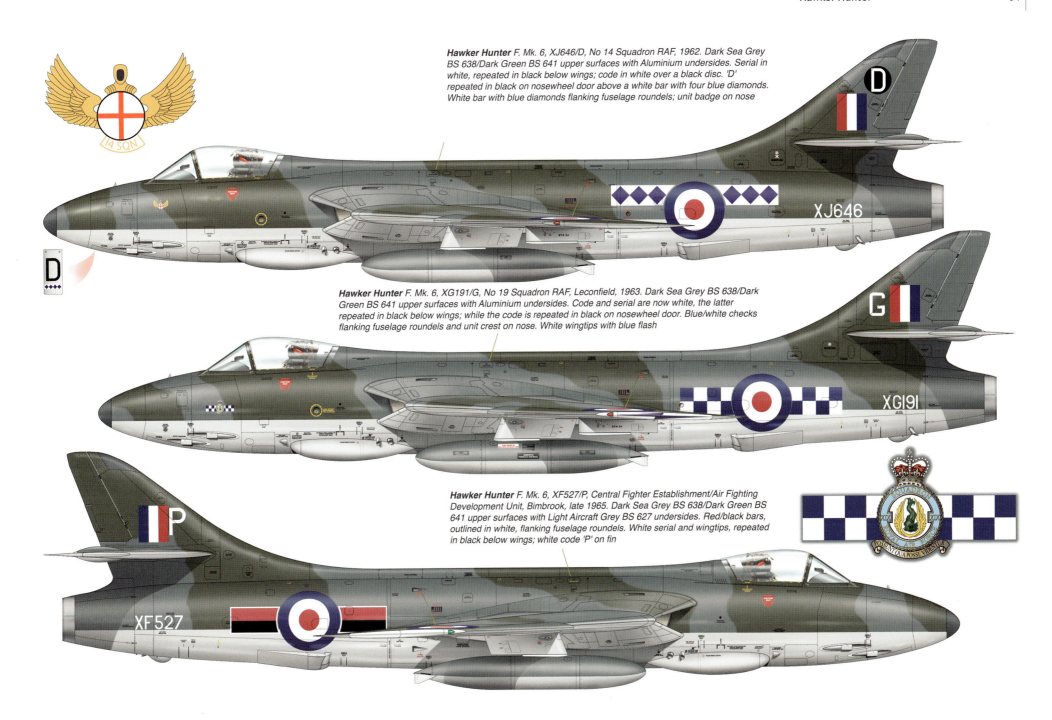

Hawker Hunter *F. Mk. 6, XJ646/D, No 14 Squadron RAF, 1962. Dark Sea Grey BS 638/Dark Green BS 641 upper surfaces with Aluminium undersides. Serial in white, repeated in black below wings; code in white over a black disc. 'D' repeated in black on nosewheel door above a white bar with four blue diamonds. White bar with blue diamonds flanking fuselage roundels; unit badge on nose*

Hawker Hunter *F. Mk. 6, XG191/G, No 19 Squadron RAF, Leconfield, 1963. Dark Sea Grey BS 638/Dark Green BS 641 upper surfaces with Aluminium undersides. Code and serial are now white, the latter repeated in black below wings; while the code is repeated in black on nosewheel door. Blue/white checks flanking fuselage roundels and unit crest on nose. White wingtips with blue flash*

Hawker Hunter *F. Mk. 6, XF527/P, Central Fighter Establishment/Air Fighting Development Unit, Bimbrook, late 1965. Dark Sea Grey BS 638/Dark Green BS 641 upper surfaces with Light Aircraft Grey BS 627 undersides. Red/black bars, outlined in white, flanking fuselage roundels. White serial and wingtips, repeated in black below wings; white code 'P' on fin*

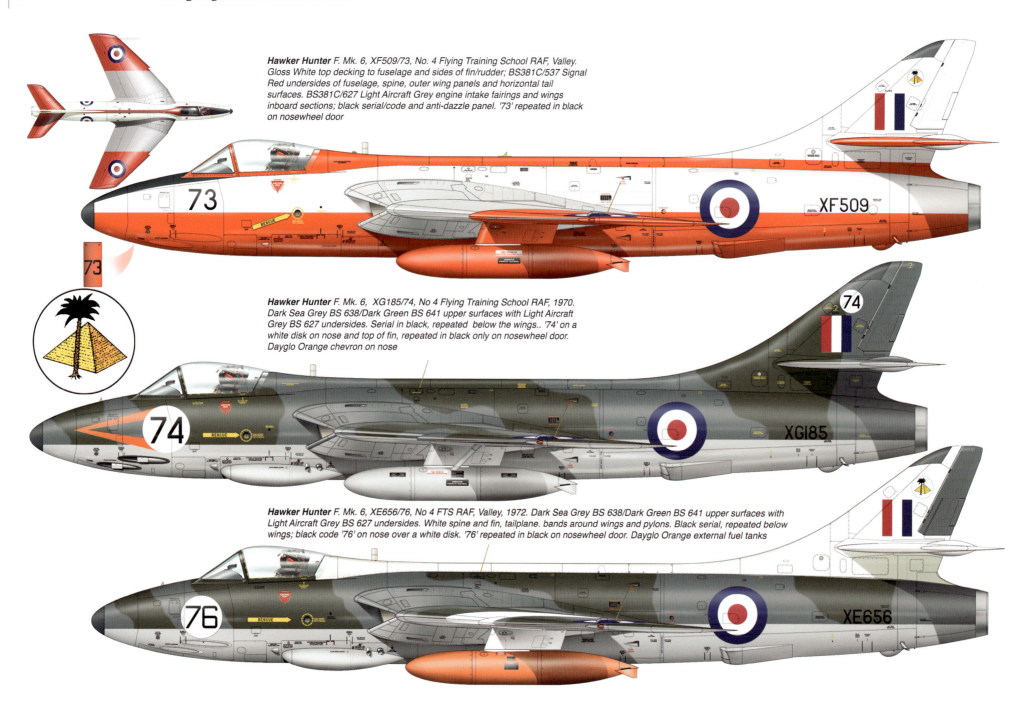

Hawker Hunter F. Mk. 6, XF509/73, No. 4 Flying Training School RAF, Valley. Gloss White top decking to fuselage and sides of fin/rudder; BS381C/537 Signal Red undersides of fuselage, spine, outer wing panels and horizontal tail surfaces. BS381C/627 Light Aircraft Grey engine intake fairings and wings inboard sections; black serial/code and anti-dazzle panel. '73' repeated in black on nosewheel door

Hawker Hunter F. Mk. 6, XG185/74, No 4 Flying Training School RAF, 1970. Dark Sea Grey BS 638/Dark Green BS 641 upper surfaces with Light Aircraft Grey BS 627 undersides. Serial in black, repeated below the wings.. '74' on a white disk on nose and top of fin, repeated in black only on nosewheel door. Dayglo Orange chevron on nose

Hawker Hunter F. Mk. 6, XE656/76, No 4 FTS RAF, Valley, 1972. Dark Sea Grey BS 638/Dark Green BS 641 upper surfaces with Light Aircraft Grey BS 627 undersides. White spine and fin, tailplane. bands around wings and pylons. Black serial, repeated below wings; black code '76' on nose over a white disk. '76' repeated in black on nosewheel door. Dayglo Orange external fuel tanks

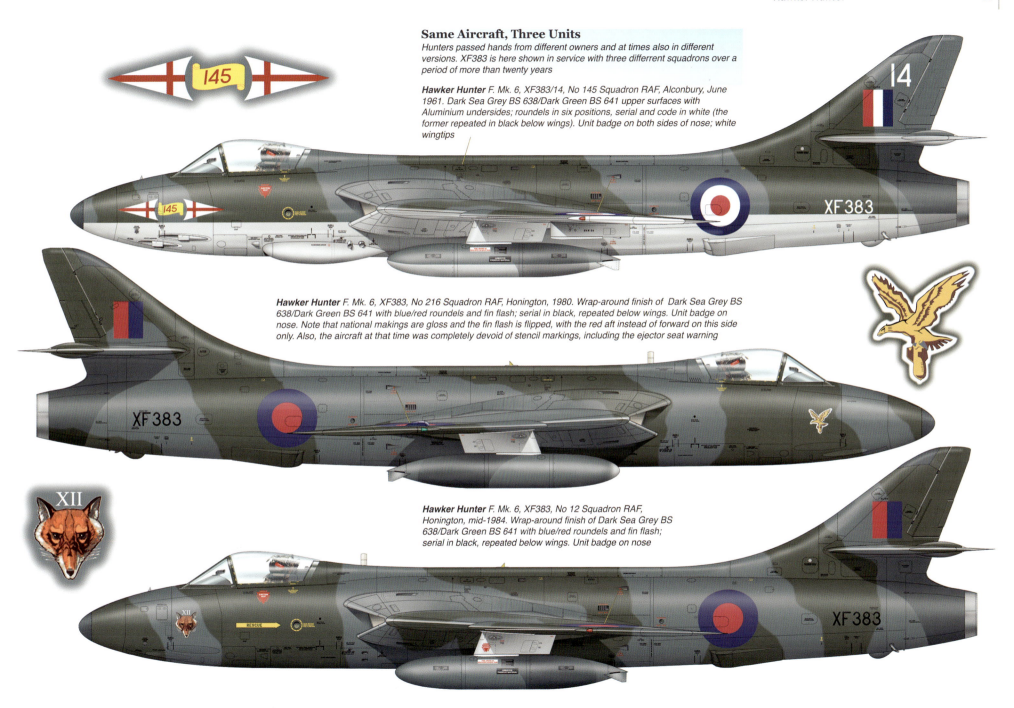

Same Aircraft, Three Units

Hunters passed hands from different owners and at times also in different versions. XF383 is here shown in service with three differrent squadrons over a period of more than twenty years

Hawker Hunter *F. Mk. 6, XF383/14, No 145 Squadron RAF, Alconbury, June 1961. Dark Sea Grey BS 638/Dark Green BS 641 upper surfaces with Aluminium undersides; roundels in six positions, serial and code in white (the former repeated in black below wings). Unit badge on both sides of nose; white wingtips*

Hawker Hunter *F. Mk. 6, XF383, No 216 Squadron RAF, Honington, 1980. Wrap-around finish of Dark Sea Grey BS 638/Dark Green BS 641 with blue/red roundels and fin flash; serial in black, repeated below wings. Unit badge on nose. Note that national makings are gloss and the fin flash is flipped, with the red aft instead of forward on this side only. Also, the aircraft at that time was completely devoid of stencil markings, including the ejector seat warning*

Hawker Hunter *F. Mk. 6, XF383, No 12 Squadron RAF, Honington, mid-1984. Wrap-around finish of Dark Sea Grey BS 638/Dark Green BS 641 with blue/red roundels and fin flash; serial in black, repeated below wings. Unit badge on nose*

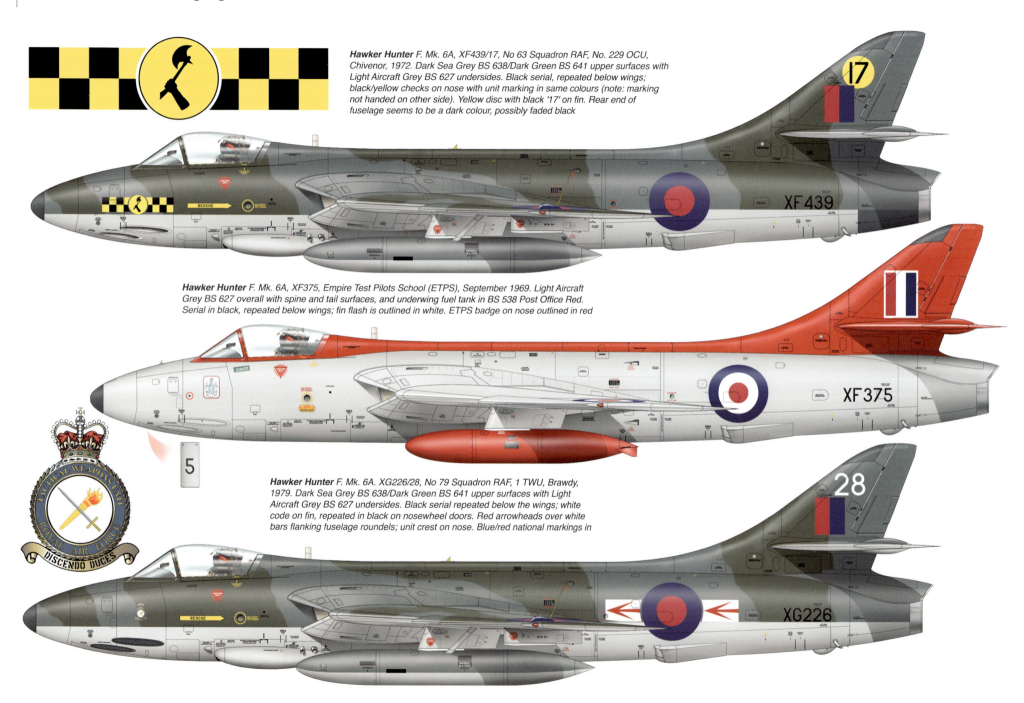

Hawker Hunter *F. Mk. 6A, XF439/17, No 63 Squadron RAF, No. 229 OCU, Chivenor, 1972. Dark Sea Grey BS 638/Dark Green BS 641 upper surfaces with Light Aircraft Grey BS 627 undersides. Black serial, repeated below wings; black/yellow checks on nose with unit marking in same colours (note: marking not handed on other side). Yellow disc with black '17' on fin. Rear end of fuselage seems to be a dark colour, possibly faded black*

Hawker Hunter *F. Mk. 6A, XF375, Empire Test Pilots School (ETPS), September 1969. Light Aircraft Grey BS 627 overall with spine and tail surfaces, and underwing fuel tank in BS 538 Post Office Red. Serial in black, repeated below wings; fin flash is outlined in white. ETPS badge on nose outlined in red*

Hawker Hunter *F. Mk. 6A. XG226/28, No 79 Squadron RAF, 1 TWU, Brawdy, 1979. Dark Sea Grey BS 638/Dark Green BS 641 upper surfaces with Light Aircraft Grey BS 627 undersides. Black serial repeated below the wings; white code on fin, repeated in black on nosewheel doors. Red arrowheads over white bars flanking fuselage roundels; unit crest on nose. Blue/red national markings in*

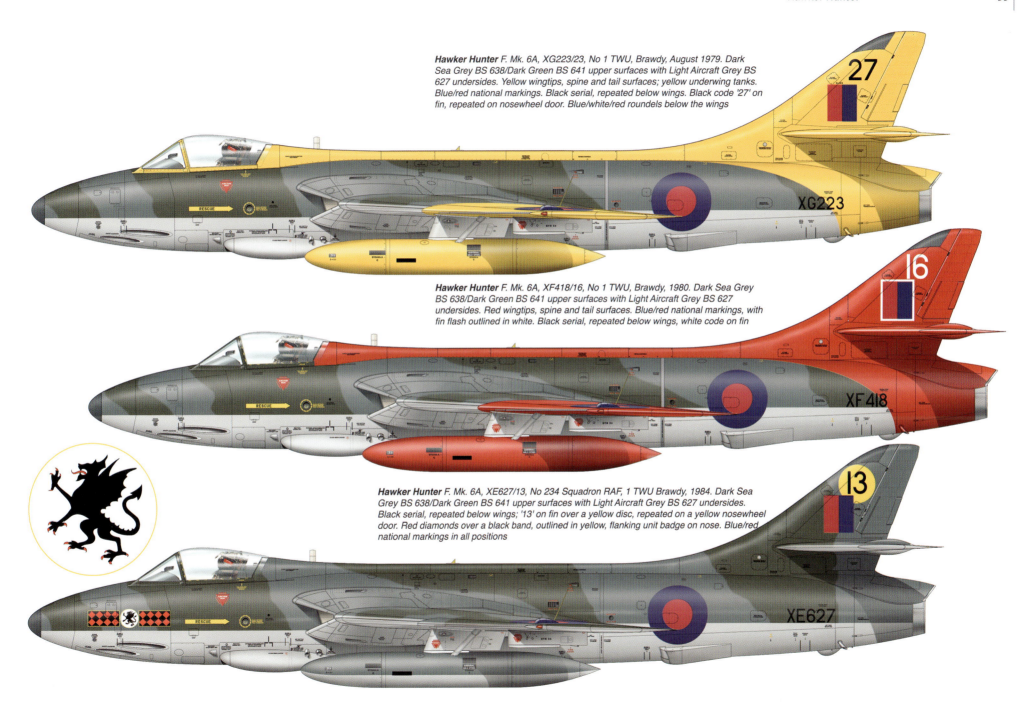

Hawker Hunter F. Mk. 6A, XG223/23, No 1 TWU, Brawdy, August 1979. Dark Sea Grey BS 638/Dark Green BS 641 upper surfaces with Light Aircraft Grey BS 627 undersides. Yellow wingtips, spine and tail surfaces; yellow underwing tanks. Blue/red national markings. Black serial, repeated below wings. Black code '27' on fin, repeated on nosewheel door. Blue/white/red roundels below the wings

Hawker Hunter F. Mk. 6A, XF418/16, No 1 TWU, Brawdy, 1980. Dark Sea Grey BS 638/Dark Green BS 641 upper surfaces with Light Aircraft Grey BS 627 undersides. Red wingtips, spine and tail surfaces. Blue/red national markings, with fin flash outlined in white. Black serial, repeated below wings, white code on fin

Hawker Hunter F. Mk. 6A, XE627/13, No 234 Squadron RAF, 1 TWU Brawdy, 1984. Dark Sea Grey BS 638/Dark Green BS 641 upper surfaces with Light Aircraft Grey BS 627 undersides. Black serial, repeated below wings; '13' on fin over a yellow disc, repeated on a yellow nosewheel door. Red diamonds over a black band, outlined in yellow, flanking unit badge on nose. Blue/red national markings in all positions

Hawker Hunter FGA. Mk. 9, XE654/LJ, flown by Squadron Leader I..A. Jones, No 8 Squadron RAF, Khormaksar, February 1963. Dark Sea Grey BS 638/Dark Green BS 641 upper surfaces with Aluminium undersides. Code and serial in white, the latter repeated in black below the wings;. Yellow-blue-red bars flanking fuselage rounbels. Note two practice concrete-head rockets under each wing. Pilot's name in white below the windscreen

Hawker Hunter FGA. Mk. 9, XE620/B, flown by Sqn Ldr Tammy Syme of No 8 Squadron RAF, detached at Embakasi, August 1963. Dark Sea Grey BS 638/Dark Green BS 641 upper surfaces with Aluminium undersides. Code and serial in white, the latter repeated in black below the wings. Pilot's name in white above rank pennant on nose. Yellow/blue/red bands flanking fuselage round, repeated on nosewheel door which also has the unit crest superimposed

Hawker Hunter FGA. Mk. 9, XE618/D, flown by Flt Lt Chris Cureton, No 8 Squadron RAF, Khormaksar. 1964. Dark Sea Grey BS 638/Dark Green BS 641 upper surfaces with Aluminium undersides. Code and serial in white, the latter repeated in black below the wings. Unit crest on nose with pilot's name in white above it. Yellow/blue/red bands flanking fuselage roundels, repeated on underwing tank. Together with XF421/C, this aircraft had received a low camouflage waistline during refurbishing at No 5 MU (RAF Kemble) the year before, but this practice was discountinued

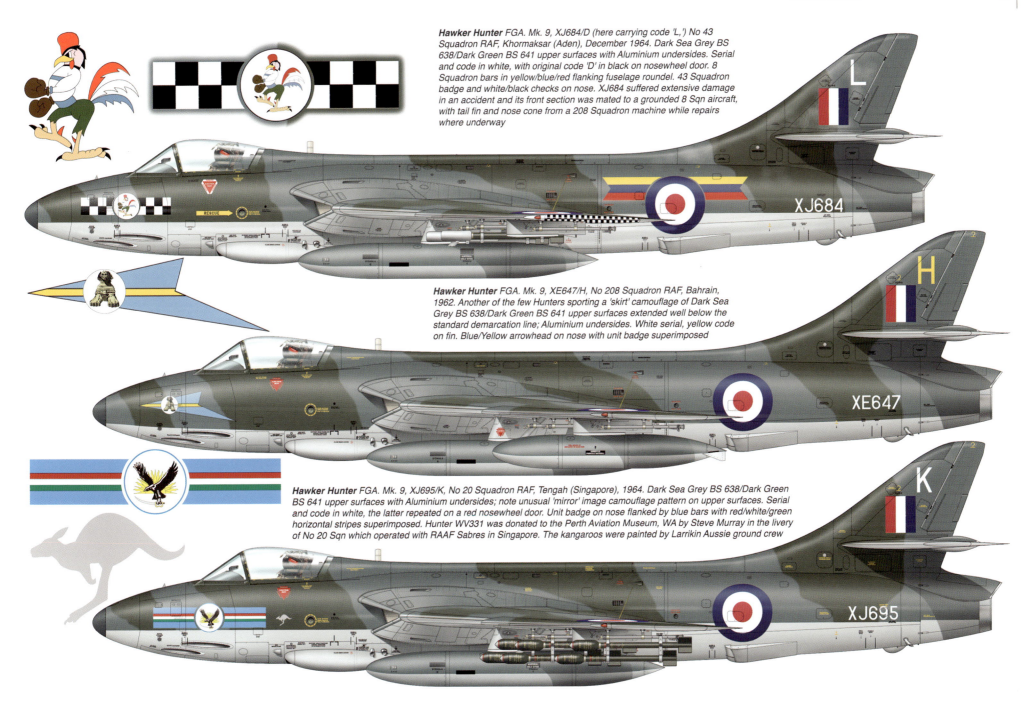

Hawker Hunter *FGA. Mk. 9, XJ684/D (here carrying code 'L,') No 43 Squadron RAF, Khormaksar (Aden), December 1964. Dark Sea Grey BS 638/Dark Green BS 641 upper surfaces with Aluminium undersides. Serial and code in white, with original code 'D' in black on nosewheel door. 8 Squadron bars in yellow/blue/red flanking fuselage roundel. 43 Squadron badge and white/black checks on nose. XJ684 suffered extensive damage in an accident and its front section was mated to a grounded 8 Sqn aircraft, with tail fin and nose cone from a 208 Squadron machine while repairs where underway*

Hawker Hunter *FGA. Mk. 9, XE647/H, No 208 Squadron RAF, Bahrain, 1962. Another of the few Hunters sporting a 'skirt' camouflage of Dark Sea Grey BS 638/Dark Green BS 641 upper surfaces extended well below the standard demarcation line; Aluminium undersides. White serial, yellow code on fin. Blue/Yellow arrowhead on nose with unit badge superimposed*

Hawker Hunter *FGA. Mk. 9, XJ695/K, No 20 Squadron RAF, Tengah (Singapore), 1964. Dark Sea Grey BS 638/Dark Green BS 641 upper surfaces with Aluminium undersides; note unusual 'mirror' image camouflage pattern on upper surfaces. Serial and code in white, the latter repeated on a red nosewheel door. Unit badge on nose flanked by blue bars with red/white/green horizontal stripes superimposed. Hunter WV331 was donated to the Perth Aviation Museum, WA by Steve Murray in the livery of No 20 Sqn which operated with RAAF Sabres in Singapore. The kangaroos were painted by Larrikin Aussie ground crew*

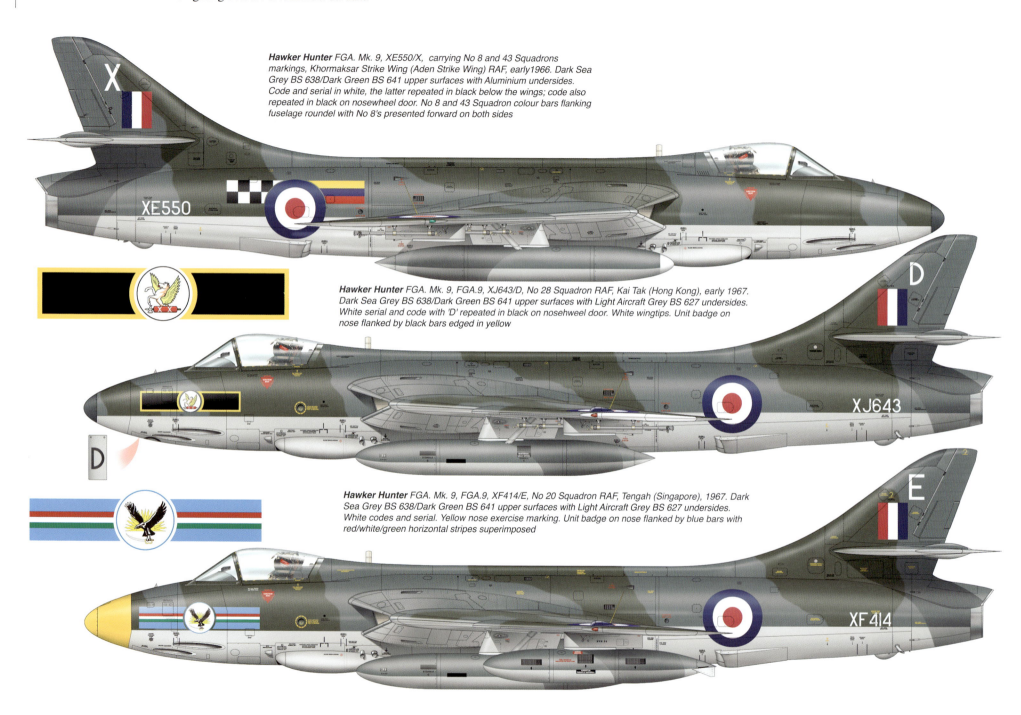

Hawker Hunter FGA. Mk. 9, XE550/X, carrying No 8 and 43 Squadrons markings, Khormaksar Strike Wing (Aden Strike Wing) RAF, early1966. Dark Sea Grey BS 638/Dark Green BS 641 upper surfaces with Aluminium undersides. Code and serial in white, the latter repeated in black below the wings; code also repeated in black on nosewheel door. No 8 and 43 Squadron colour bars flanking fuselage roundel with No 8's presented forward on both sides

Hawker Hunter FGA. Mk. 9, FGA.9, XJ643/D, No 28 Squadron RAF, Kai Tak (Hong Kong), early 1967. Dark Sea Grey BS 638/Dark Green BS 641 upper surfaces with Light Aircraft Grey BS 627 undersides. White serial and code with 'D' repeated in black on nosehweel door. White wingtips. Unit badge on nose flanked by black bars edged in yellow

Hawker Hunter FGA. Mk. 9, FGA.9, XF414/E, No 20 Squadron RAF, Tengah (Singapore), 1967. Dark Sea Grey BS 638/Dark Green BS 641 upper surfaces with Light Aircraft Grey BS 627 undersides. White codes and serial. Yellow nose exercise marking. Unit badge on nose flanked by blue bars with red/white/green horizontal stripes superimposed

Hawker Hunter FGA. Mk. 9, XJ642/L, No 54 Squadron RAF, June 1968. High Gloss Dark Sea Grey BS 638/Dark Green BS 641 upper surfaces with BS 627 Gloss Light Aircraft Grey undersides. Black serial, yellow code on fin repeated in black on nose wheel door. Badge on nose flanked by yellow/blue checks. White wingtips

Hawker Hunter FGA. Mk. 9, XJ691/G, No 208 Squadron RAF, 1968. Dark Sea Grey BS 638/Dark Green BS 641 upper surfaces with Light Aircraft Grey BS 627 undersides. White serial, yellow code on fin, repeated in black on nosewheel door. Unit badge in a white disk over a light blue and yellow flash, on nose and on front of inner underwing fuel tank

Hawker Hunter FGA. Mk. 9, XJ636/F, No 208 Squadron RAF, Muharraq (Aden), 1968. Dark Sea Grey BS 638/Dark Green BS 641 upper surfaces with Light Aircraft Grey BS 627 undersides. Black serial, yellow code on fin. Light blue/yellow bars flanking fuselage roundel, outlined in black (or possibly dark blue)

Hawker Hunter *FGA. Mk. 9, XE624/B, No 1 Squadron RAF, West Raynham, 1968. Dark Sea Grey BS 638/Dark Green BS 641 upper surfaces with Light Aircraft Grey BS 627 undersides. Unit badge on nose with pilot's name, Flt Lt A.R. Pollock in white above; a white 'Tower Bridge' is also painted aft. Code 'B' on fin in white, thinly outlined in red, repeated on nosewheel door in black. White wingtips. Pollock performed the daring flight under Tower Bridge in Hunter XF442/H on 4 April 1968*

Hawker Hunter *FGA. Mk. 9, XK137/66, No. 45 Squadron RAF, Wittering, 1974. Dark Sea Grey BS 638/Dark Green BS 641 upper surfaces with Light Aircraft Grey BS 627 undersides. Blue/red roundels on fuselage sides and above wings, no markings under the wings. Code '66' in white on fin, repeated in black on nosewheel door; serial in black. Note squadron marking on nose thinly outlined in light blue*

Hawker Hunter *FGA. Mk. 9, XG228/56, No 79 Squadron RAF, 1 TWU, Brawdy, September 1973. Dark Sea Grey BS 638/Dark Green BS 641 upper surfaces with Light Aircraft Grey BS 627 undersides. Black serial repeated below the wings; white code on fin, repeated in black on nosewheel doors. Red arrowheads over white bars flanking fuselage roundels; unit crest on nose. Blue/red national markings in all positions*

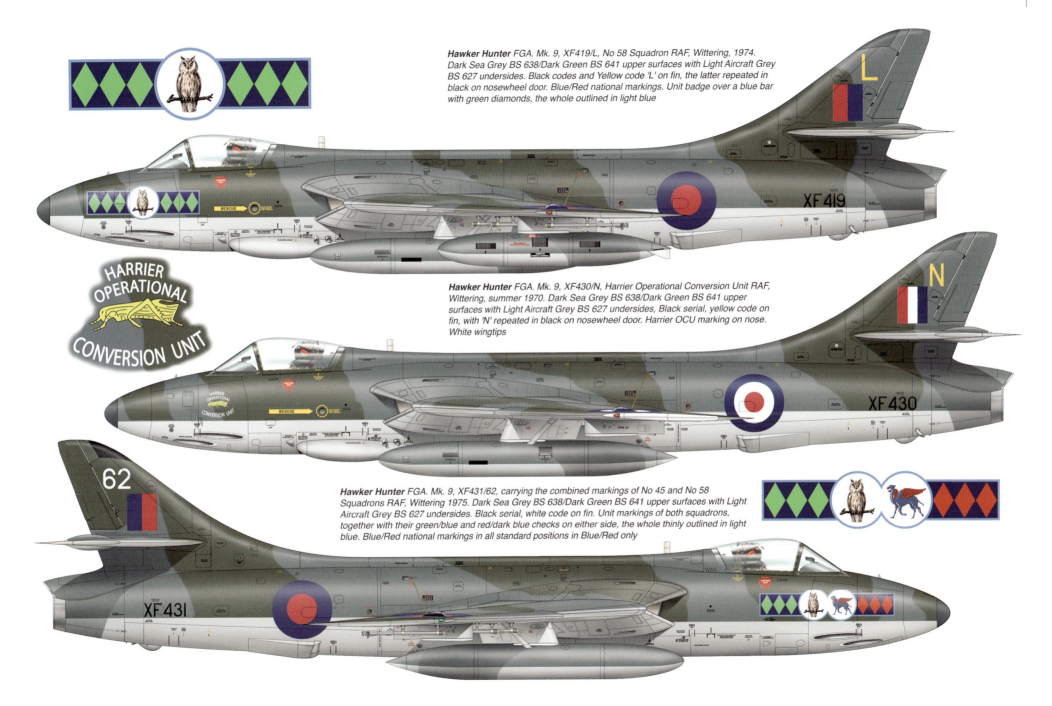

Hawker Hunter *FGA. Mk. 9, XF419/L, No 58 Squadron RAF, Wittering, 1974. Dark Sea Grey BS 638/Dark Green BS 641 upper surfaces with Light Aircraft Grey BS 627 undersides. Black codes and Yellow code 'L' on fin, the latter repeated in black on nosewheel door. Blue/Red national markings. Unit badge over a blue bar with green diamonds, the whole outlined in light blue*

Hawker Hunter *FGA. Mk. 9, XF430/N, Harrier Operational Conversion Unit RAF, Wittering, summer 1970. Dark Sea Grey BS 638/Dark Green BS 641 upper surfaces with Light Aircraft Grey BS 627 undersides, Black serial, yellow code on fin, with 'N' repeated in black on nosewheel door. Harrier OCU marking on nose. White wingtips*

Hawker Hunter *FGA. Mk. 9, XF431/62, carrying the combined markings of No 45 and No 58 Squadrons RAF, Wittering 1975. Dark Sea Grey BS 638/Dark Green BS 641 upper surfaces with Light Aircraft Grey BS 627 undersides. Black serial, white code on fin. Unit markings of both squadrons, together with their green/blue and red/dark blue checks on either side, the whole thinly outlined in light blue. Blue/Red national markings in all standard positions in Blue/Red only*

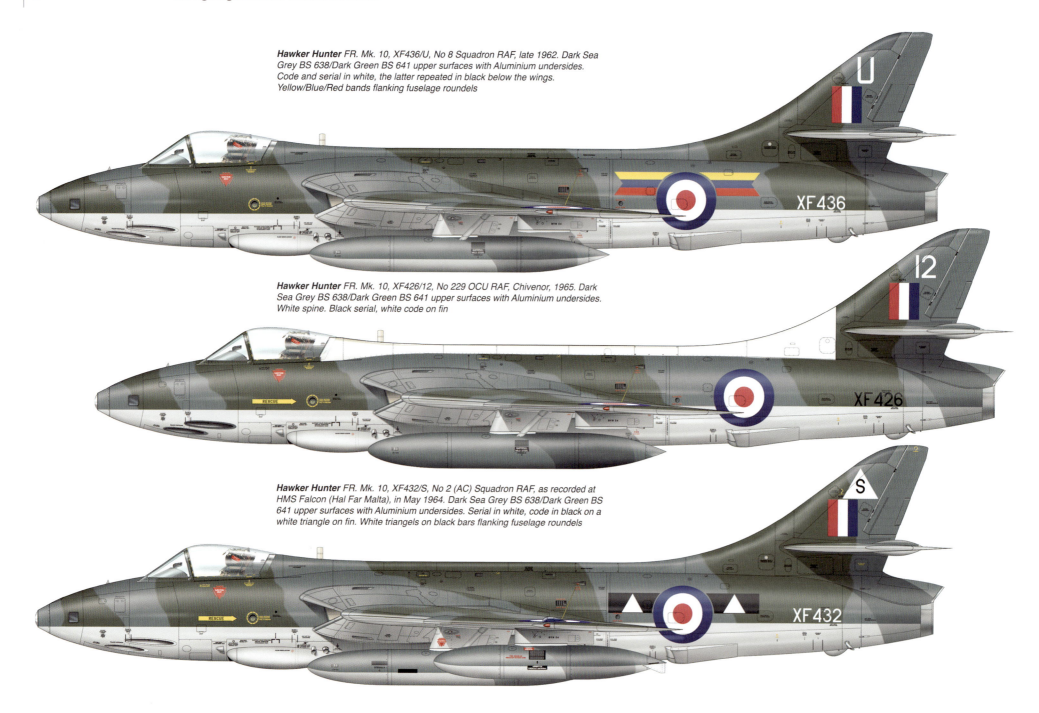

Hawker Hunter FR. Mk. 10, XF436/U, No 8 Squadron RAF, late 1962. Dark Sea Grey BS 638/Dark Green BS 641 upper surfaces with Aluminium undersides. Code and serial in white, the latter repeated in black below the wings. Yellow/Blue/Red bands flanking fuselage roundels

Hawker Hunter FR. Mk. 10, XF426/12, No 229 OCU RAF, Chivenor, 1965. Dark Sea Grey BS 638/Dark Green BS 641 upper surfaces with Aluminium undersides. White spine. Black serial, white code on fin

Hawker Hunter FR. Mk. 10, XF432/S, No 2 (AC) Squadron RAF, as recorded at HMS Falcon (Hal Far Malta), in May 1964. Dark Sea Grey BS 638/Dark Green BS 641 upper surfaces with Aluminium undersides. Serial in white, code in black on a white triangle on fin. White triangels on black bars flanking fuselage roundels

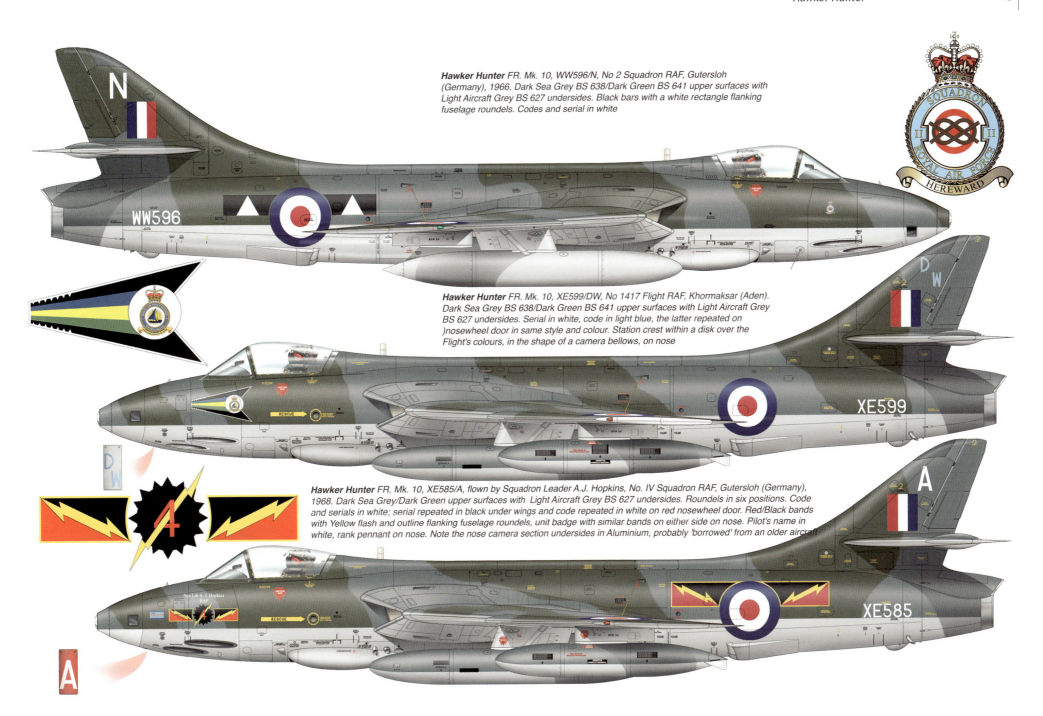

Hawker Hunter FR. Mk. 10, WW596/N, No 2 Squadron RAF, Gutersloh (Germany), 1966. Dark Sea Grey BS 638/Dark Green BS 641 upper surfaces with Light Aircraft Grey BS 627 undersides. Black bars with a white rectangle flanking fuselage roundels. Codes and serial in white

Hawker Hunter FR. Mk. 10, XE599/DW, No 1417 Flight RAF, Khormaksar (Aden). Dark Sea Grey BS 638/Dark Green BS 641 upper surfaces with Light Aircraft Grey BS 627 undersides. Serial in white, code in light blue, the latter repeated on)nosewheel door in same style and colour. Station crest within a disk over the Flight's colours, in the shape of a camera bellows, on nose

Hawker Hunter FR. Mk. 10, XE585/A, flown by Squadron Leader A.J. Hopkins, No. IV Squadron RAF, Gutersloh (Germany), 1968. Dark Sea Grey/Dark Green upper surfaces with Light Aircraft Grey BS 627 undersides. Roundels in six positions. Code and serials in white; serial repeated in black under wings and code repeated in white on red nosewheel door. Red/Black bands with Yellow flash and outline flanking fuselage roundels, unit badge with similar bands on either side on nose. Pilot's name in white, rank pennant on nose. Note the nose camera section undersides in Aluminium, probably 'borrowed' from an older aircraft

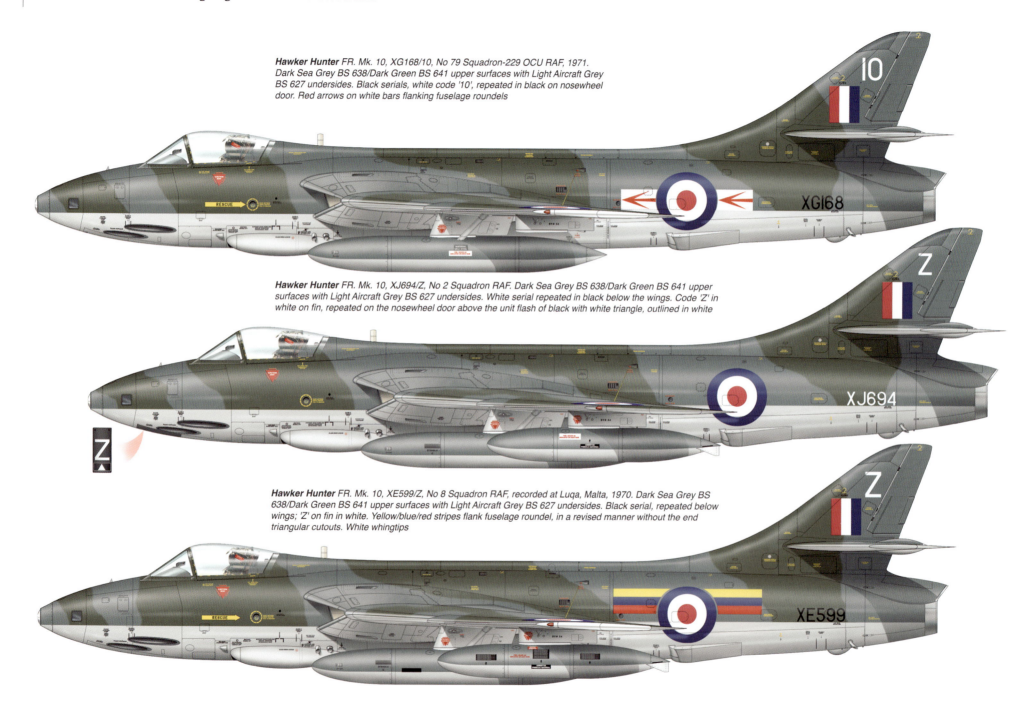

Hawker Hunter FR. Mk. 10, XG168/10, No 79 Squadron-229 OCU RAF, 1971. Dark Sea Grey BS 638/Dark Green BS 641 upper surfaces with Light Aircraft Grey BS 627 undersides. Black serials, white code '10', repeated in black on nosewheel door. Red arrows on white bars flanking fuselage roundels

Hawker Hunter FR. Mk. 10, XJ694/Z, No 2 Squadron RAF. Dark Sea Grey BS 638/Dark Green BS 641 upper surfaces with Light Aircraft Grey BS 627 undersides. White serial repeated in black below the wings. Code 'Z' in white on fin, repeated on the nosewheel door above the unit flash of black with white triangle, outlined in white

Hawker Hunter FR. Mk. 10, XE599/Z, No 8 Squadron RAF, recorded at Luqa, Malta, 1970. Dark Sea Grey BS 638/Dark Green BS 641 upper surfaces with Light Aircraft Grey BS 627 undersides. Black serial, repeated below wings; 'Z' on fin in white. Yellow/blue/red stripes flank fuselage roundel, in a revised manner without the end triangular cutouts. White whingtips

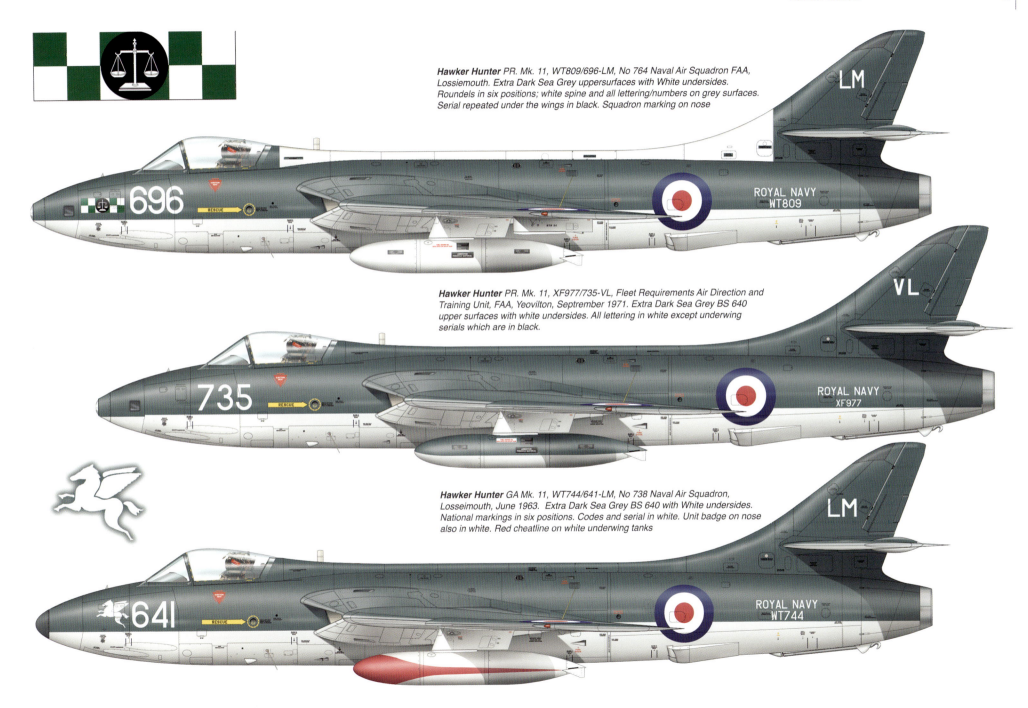

Hawker Hunter *PR. Mk. 11, WT809/696-LM, No 764 Naval Air Squadron FAA, Lossiemouth. Extra Dark Sea Grey uppersurfaces with White undersides. Roundels in six positions; white spine and all lettering/numbers on grey surfaces. Serial repeated under the wings in black. Squadron marking on nose*

Hawker Hunter *PR. Mk. 11, XF977/735-VL, Fleet Requirements Air Direction and Training Unit, FAA, Yeovilton, Septrember 1971. Extra Dark Sea Grey BS 640 upper surfaces with white undersides. All lettering in white except underwing serials which are in black.*

Hawker Hunter *GA Mk. 11, WT744/641-LM, No 738 Naval Air Squadron, Losseimouth, June 1963. Extra Dark Sea Grey BS 640 with White undersides. National markings in six positions. Codes and serial in white. Unit badge on nose also in white. Red cheatline on white underwing tanks*

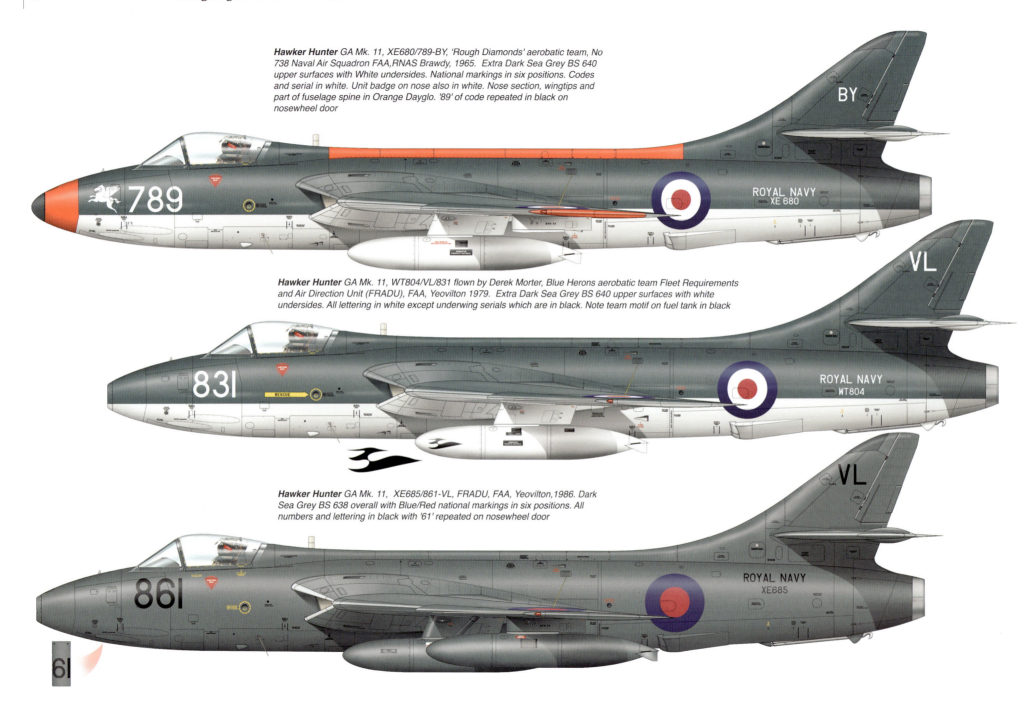

Hawker Hunter GA Mk. 11, XE680/789-BY, 'Rough Diamonds' aerobatic team, No 738 Naval Air Squadron FAA,RNAS Brawdy, 1965. Extra Dark Sea Grey BS 640 upper surfaces with White undersides. National markings in six positions. Codes and serial in white. Unit badge on nose also in white. Nose section, wingtips and part of fuselage spine in Orange Dayglo. '89' of code repeated in black on nosewheel door

Hawker Hunter GA Mk. 11, WT804/VL/831 flown by Derek Morter, Blue Herons aerobatic team Fleet Requirements and Air Direction Unit (FRADU), FAA, Yeovilton 1979. Extra Dark Sea Grey BS 640 upper surfaces with white undersides. All lettering in white except underwing serials which are in black. Note team motif on fuel tank in black

Hawker Hunter GA Mk. 11, XE685/861-VL, FRADU, FAA, Yeovilton,1986. Dark Sea Grey BS 638 overall with Blue/Red national markings in six positions. All numbers and lettering in black with '61' repeated on nosewheel door

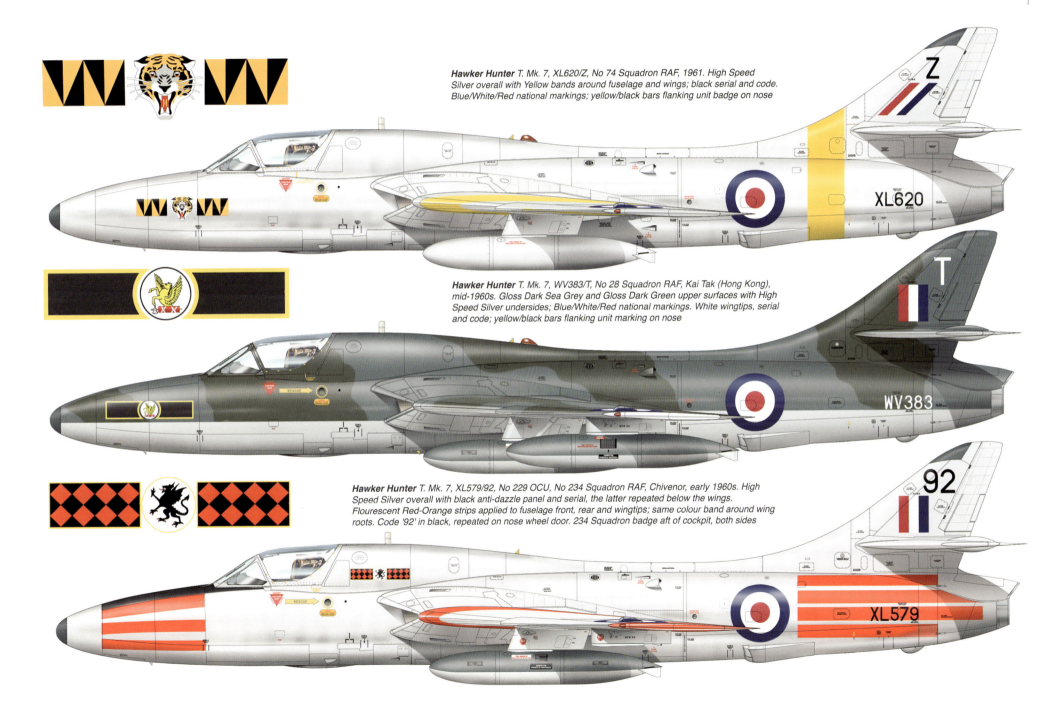

Hawker Hunter T. Mk. 7, XL620/Z, No 74 Squadron RAF, 1961. High Speed Silver overall with Yellow bands around fuselage and wings; black serial and code. Blue/White/Red national markings; yellow/black bars flanking unit badge on nose

Hawker Hunter T. Mk. 7, WV383/T, No 28 Squadron RAF, Kai Tak (Hong Kong), mid-1960s. Gloss Dark Sea Grey and Gloss Dark Green upper surfaces with High Speed Silver undersides; Blue/White/Red national markings. White wingtips, serial and code; yellow/black bars flanking unit marking on nose

Hawker Hunter T. Mk. 7, XL579/92, No 229 OCU, No 234 Squadron RAF, Chivenor, early 1960s. High Speed Silver overall with black anti-dazzle panel and serial, the latter repeated below the wings. Flourescent Red-Orange strips applied to fuselage front, rear and wingtips; same colour band around wing roots. Code '92' in black, repeated on nose wheel door. 234 Squadron badge aft of cockpit, both sides

Hawker Hunter *T. Mk. 7, XL566/TW, No 1417 Flight RAF, Khormaksar (Aden), 1967. Dark Sea Grey BS 638/Dark Green BS 641 upper surfaces with Light Aircraft Grey BS 627 undersides.; White wingtips. Serial in white, repeated below the wings in black. Codes on fin in yellow. No 8 and 43 Squadron colour bars flanking fuselage roundel with No 8's presented forward on both sides. Unit badge on nose*

Hawker Hunter *T. Mk. 7, XL596/I, No IV (AC) Squadron RAF, Wildenrath (Germany), September 1970. High Speed Silver overall with black anti-dazzle panel and serial, the latter repeated below the wings. Flourescent Red-Orange strips applied to fuselage front, rear and wingtips; same colour band around wing roots. Serial 'I' in black, repeated on nose wheel door. unit badge on front fuselage, both sides. Note inner fuel tank in Medium Sea Grey overall while the outer tank is in Dark Sea Grey over Light Aircraft Grey*

Hawker Hunter *T. Mk. 7, WV383, Royal Aircraft Establishment, 1972. Light Aircraft Grey overall with Blue vertical tail surfaces (including bullet fairing), wingtips, part of external fuel tank and nose flash; black anti-dazzle panel. Black serial; Blue/White/Red national markings, with fin flash outlined in white. RAE crest aft of cockpit*

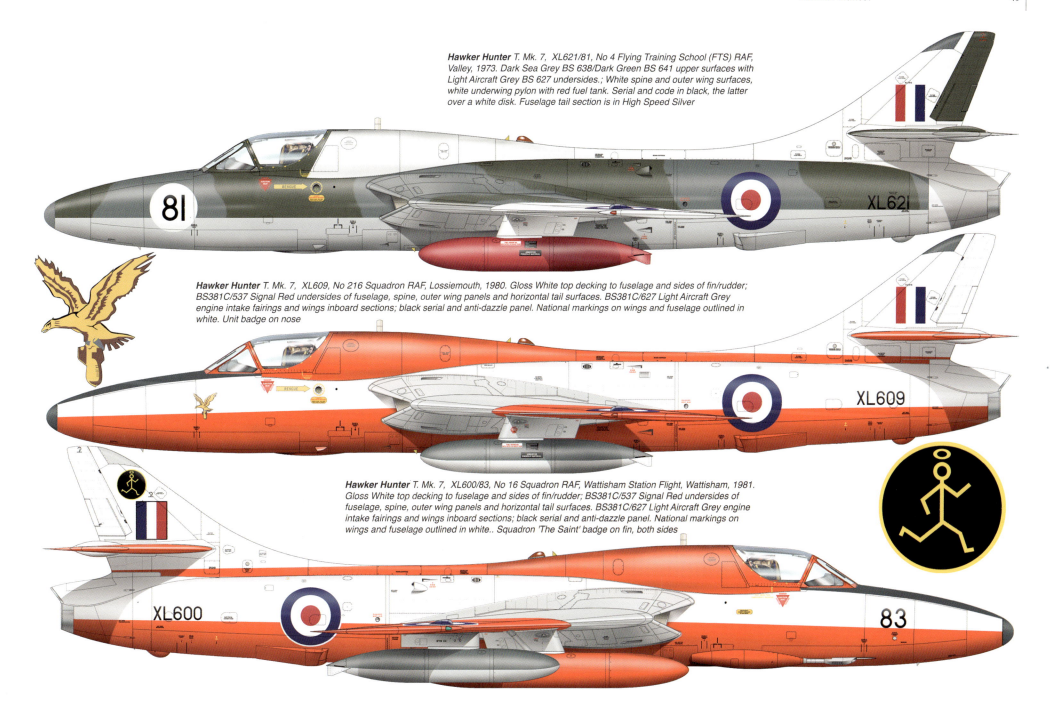

Hawker Hunter T. Mk. 7, XL621/81, No 4 Flying Training School (FTS) RAF, Valley, 1973. Dark Sea Grey BS 638/Dark Green BS 641 upper surfaces with Light Aircraft Grey BS 627 undersides.; White spine and outer wing surfaces, white underwing pylon with red fuel tank. Serial and code in black, the latter over a white disk. Fuselage tail section is in High Speed Silver

Hawker Hunter T. Mk. 7, XL609, No 216 Squadron RAF, Lossiemouth, 1980. Gloss White top decking to fuselage and sides of fin/rudder; BS381C/537 Signal Red undersides of fuselage, spine, outer wing panels and horizontal tail surfaces. BS381C/627 Light Aircraft Grey engine intake fairings and wings inboard sections; black serial and anti-dazzle panel. National markings on wings and fuselage outlined in white. Unit badge on nose

Hawker Hunter T. Mk. 7, XL600/83, No 16 Squadron RAF, Wattisham Station Flight, Wattisham, 1981. Gloss White top decking to fuselage and sides of fin/rudder; BS381C/537 Signal Red undersides of fuselage, spine, outer wing panels and horizontal tail surfaces. BS381C/627 Light Aircraft Grey engine intake fairings and wings inboard sections; black serial and anti-dazzle panel. National markings on wings and fuselage outlined in white.. Squadron 'The Saint' badge on fin, both sides

Hawker Hunter T. Mk. 7, WV318/M, No 208 Squadron RAF, 1986. Dark Sea Grey/Dark Green upper surfaces with Light Aircraft Grey undersides; Blue/Red national markings. Black serial, light blue code on fin; yellow/blue arrowhead on nose, unit markings on fin

Hawker Hunter T. Mk. 7, XL613/CU, No 237 Operational Conversion Unit RAF, 1985. Dark Sea Grey/Dark Green upper surfaces with Light Aircraft Grey undersides; Blue/Red national markings. Black serial, black code on fin thickly outlined in white; unit badge on nose

Hawker Hunter T. Mk. 7, XL573/573, No 12 Squadron RAF, Lossiemouth, early 1980s. Dark Sea Grey BS 638 and Dark Green BS 641 wrap round camouflage. Light Aircraft Grey underwing pylons and Dark Sea Grey/Light Aircraft Grey fuel tanks. Unit badge on nose

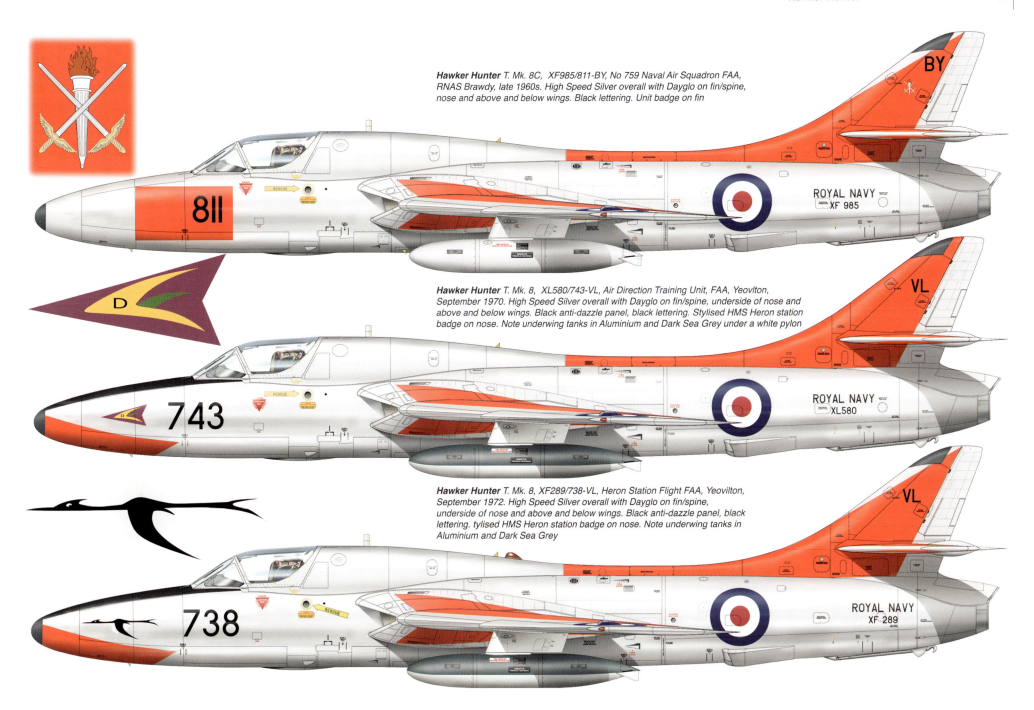

Hawker Hunter *T. Mk. 8C, XF985/811-BY, No 759 Naval Air Squadron FAA, RNAS Brawdy, late 1960s. High Speed Silver overall with Dayglo on fin/spine, nose and above and below wings. Black lettering. Unit badge on fin*

Hawker Hunter *T. Mk. 8, XL580/743-VL, Air Direction Training Unit, FAA, Yeovlton, September 1970. High Speed Silver overall with Dayglo on fin/spine, underside of nose and above and below wings. Black anti-dazzle panel, black lettering. Stylised HMS Heron station badge on nose. Note underwing tanks in Aluminium and Dark Sea Grey under a white pylon*

Hawker Hunter *T. Mk. 8, XF289/738-VL, Heron Station Flight FAA, Yeovilton, September 1972. High Speed Silver overall with Dayglo on fin/spine, underside of nose and above and below wings. Black anti-dazzle panel, black lettering. tylised HMS Heron station badge on nose. Note underwing tanks in Aluminium and Dark Sea Grey*

Hawker Hunter T. Mk. 8C, XF985/877-VL, Fleet Requirements and Air Direction Unit (FRADU), Yeovilton, April 1989. Dark Sea Grey BS 638 overall with Blue/Red national markings in six positions. All numbers and lettering in black with '77' repeated on nosewheel door White air intake lips. Note inboard undewing tank in 'RAF style' Dark Sea Grey/Light Aircraft Grey finish

Hawker Hunter T. Mk. 8M, XL580/719-VL, No 899 Naval Air Squadron, FAA, Yeovilton, June 1985. Extra Dark Sea Grey BS 640 uppersurfaces with White undersides. Roundels in six positions; white lettering/numbers on grey surfaces. Serial repeated under the wings in black. 'flying fist' marking in white and black on fin

Hawker Hunter T. Mk. 8M, XL603/724, No 899 Naval Air Squadron FAA, Yeovilton, late 1980s. Dark Sea Grey BS 638 overall with Blue/Red national markings in six positions. All numbers and lettering in black with '24' repeated on nosewheel door. White air intake lips. 'flying fist' motif on fin in black and white